GREAT MENUS

Seasonal Recipes for Entertaining

GREAT MENUS

Seasonal Recipes for Entertaining

Patricia Lewis Mote

Photography David Harp
Food Styling Carlotta Botvin
Book Design Melissa Robinson

DICMAR Publishers
Washington DC

Published by
DICMAR Publishing
Washington, DC
www.dicmar.com

Book Design by
Melissa Robinson

ISBN: 978-0-933165-17-5

Printed in China
through
Four Colour Print Group,
Louisville, Kentucky

First edition

FSC
Mixed Sources
Product group from well-managed
forests and other controlled sources
Cert no. SGS-COC-003563
www.fsc.org
© 1996 Forest Stewardship Council

So Many People To Thank

For the last 12 years I have been working with many terrific people at the University of Maryland. They have been inspiring to me and have fueled the creative juices. To begin, my wonderful assistant Stephen Oetkin who never failed me in the "let's put on a party" mode, our fabulous Chef Tom Schraa from whom I learned so much, and Carlotta Botvin one of the most creative persons I know.

This book is filled with food shared with friends over the years, here are just a few special people:

Melinda and Ralph Mendelson for editing and faith
Lady Barbara Kwiatkowski for being a role model for living and
    caring
Bob and Donna Oliver for recipes and support
Cynthia Howes for the best brownie recipe
Sue Randall for her Oyster puffs
Bob and Kathy Piziali for tasting and tasting for ever
Our super daughter and son who married people who like my
    cooking, especially Consie for testing and editing
4 adorable grandchildren for whom I always love to cook

And most of all, thank you to my husband Dan for giving me everything worth having.

TABLE OF CONTENTS

Introduction

I love to cook! I cannot think of anything that gives me greater pleasure than cooking for my family and friends. What is better than gathering around you those that you love and sharing a space in time?

My fascination with cooking started early. My grandmother would make lunch every weekday for the 8 men who worked in my grandfather's forge in L.A. By the age of 5, I was "helping". We are not talking sandwiches- these were full meals; fried pork chops, mashed potatoes and pan gravy, biscuits, green beans, pies, and my favorite-salads. WOW! A lot of calories for those heavy workers. The only concession to beauty was the gaily-checked oilcloth on the table. How times have changed.

Maybe it is the artist in me, but the perfect meal not only has food that tastes delicious, but the food and the table should look beautiful. It is the whole package, and I adore putting it together. It is like giving your friends a present.

Shopping for the freshest ingredients rewards me with the best results, so shopping is important. Enter into the spirit of it and you will have great meals. A wonderful way I get involved in the process is to go to a farmers' market, wander around looking at all the glorious food and talking to the purveyors. They are all so proud of their products. There is no doubt that fresh makes an enormous difference. It is not always possible to get foods just out of the ground and off the vine but I have found that it pays to try to find them.

All of the menus in "Great Menus" are for the home cook arranged around the four seasons, and most of the ingredients are available in season. Many foods are now available year round and I do use some of them. Of course, unless we live in the tropics we are never going to have mangos or pineapples in the farmers' markets, but we can make an effort to buy as locally and sustainably as possible.

The first total dinner I ever cooked was the summer I turned 13. My family along with my favorite aunt and uncle were at a fishing cabin on the Rouge River in Oregon. It was called "Fly Fisherman's Flop". How could I forget a name like that!

Here is the Menu:

Tillamook Cheese and Crackers
Freshly Caught Pan Fried Rainbow Trout
Biscuits
Everything Salad
Just Picked Blackberry Crisp a la Mode

The one thing that I do remember very clearly was that the "kitchen" was about 6'x 6' and the temperature in there was about 110 degrees. My aunt kept saying," poor little thing". I know that I was red in the face and dripping, but happy and proud.

All of the recipes marked with an * are in the Basics section of the book. These are items that appear more than once in the cookbook.

I hope that you will find that 'Great Menus' gives you the confidence to cook for your friends and family with pride and joy. Cook whatever makes you and yours happy.

Don't forget to have fun!

Patsy

1

Items in the menus followed by an asterisk* you will find in this section

Buying Fresh Fish

As our seas become more depleted, we must become vigilant in the seafood we buy. If your local fishmonger does not label the origin of their fish, the Monterey Bay Aquarium has a web site where you can find which fish are most sustainable. They have a hand book and they even have an app.

Local and Sustainable Produce

I do try to keep to local and sustainable but some items do pop up in my recipes, like grapes and celery; I didn't even think about celery having a season until we lived in England. The items I always have are lemons, limes, onions and garlic. Many areas now grow hydroponic tomatoes which give you the look of a tomato if not the promise.

Pantry

Cholula: I love this hot sauce and so do a lot of chefs I know. It has just the proper amount of kick without overpowering the flavor of the other ingredients.

Hoisin Sauce: I think that the "Koon Chun" brand makes the best Chinese condiments. Their Plum Sauce is also delicious. Try it on pork tenderloins.

Olive Oils: I usually have 2 types, an extra virgin for salads, and regular for cooking.

Oregon White Truffle Oil: Many truffle oils are actually made with chemicals not the real thing. This is the real thing.

Narsai's Chocolate Decadence Sauce: This wonderful sauce turns the ordinary into the extraordinary. Get it on line at Narsai.com.

Pasta: My favorite brand of dry pasta is De Cecco.

Rice Vinegar: I like the Murukan line with all natural ingredients. Rice vinegar has less acid than regular vinegar. It is perfect to use for salads of baby lettuce, especially when served with fruit.

Smoked Paprika: This is another case where the brand really makes a difference. "Safinter" makes a smoked Spanish paprika that makes every thing else just seem like red powder.

Tomatoes: San Marzano puréed tomatoes really do make the best sauce. Several brands from Italy use these tomatoes. Muir Glen and Pomi are also good. Pomi is not in a can and keeps better after being opened.

Turbinado Sugar: This is an organic raw cane sugar that has been steam cleaned. It has a hint of molasses flavor.

Basic Recipes

1 lb. almonds
1 T olive oil
2 t sea salt
1 t paprika
1 t cumin

Roasted Almonds:
Blanch almonds in boiling water for 1 minute, remove from water and while still warm pop off the skin. Heat olive oil in a frying pan, then add remaining ingredients. Cook stirring until golden. Be careful as they burn easily. These will keep for a couple of days.

Bread Crumbs:
In the food processor grind the bread into not too fine crumbs. Place on a baking sheet and bake at 300° for 10 minutes; shaking the crumbs half-way through. Baking keeps the crumbs from getting moldy. If you need finer crumbs simply regrind.

2 whole chickens to give you;
2 backs
4 wings
rib bones from the breast
2 necks
Then add:
2 coarsely chopped onions
2 chopped carrots
4 stalks celery
1 chopped turnip
1 bay leaf
6 pepper corns
2 sprigs parsley
1 sprig thyme

5 egg yolks
1/3 cup sugar
2 cups scalded whole milk
1 t vanilla extract

1½ cups sifted flour
4 large eggs
1 cup milk
1 cup water
4 T melted butter
(1 T sugar for sweet crèpes)

Chicken Stock:

We had a family friend who had a wonderful Chinese cook. Wing made the best soups ever; I learned it was all in the broth. He always had a stock pot going. Most of us won't do that, but I do make homemade chicken broth at least once a month and freeze what I do not use right away. I buy whole chickens and cut them up. If you roast a chicken add all the bones left from that.

Put it all in a pot and cover with water. Let the stock simmer gently for a couple of hours. Let it cool and then drain into another pot through a colander pressing down to get all the juice out of the vegetables. Let cool overnight and remove the fat from the top. The stock should be jelly like. Bring to a boil and then salt the broth. Strain through a fine sieve. Use or freeze within a day.

Crème Anglaise:

In the top of a double boiler, beat the yolks and sugar with a wire whisk until thick. Add in the milk slowly and then place the top pan over barely simmering water. Stir with a wooden spoon until the custard coats the spoon. This takes about 3 minutes. Do not let the temperature go over 175˚ on your candy thermometer or you will have scrambled eggs. Take off the heat, and stir in the vanilla. Stir until cool. Place in a bowl and place plastic wrap directly on the custard. It will hold for 3 days.

Crèpes:

Put into a blender flour, eggs, milk, water and butter. Mix and let sit at least 1 hour or refrigerate overnight. Ladle 1/4 cup of batter into an eight inch well seasoned crèpe pan. I have a small ladle which works well. Cook the crèpe until the edges turn golden, turn over and cook for another 3 seconds. These keep for several hours or overnight; or you may freeze them.
To freeze: Brush each crèpe with melted butter and stack between sheets of wax paper; this makes them easier to separate. Package the crèpes in a freezer baggie.

1 cup chopped parsley
4 T lemon zest
2 cloves grated garlic
sea salt and pepper

8 oz. package softened cream cheese
5 oz. chèvre
1 small finely diced shallot
1 minced clove of garlic
1 T each of finely chopped dill, chives, and parsley
¼ t ground pepper
salt

6 large egg whites at room temperature
1 ¼ cup sugar
1 T corn starch
1 t lemon juice
1 t vanilla

Gremolata:
An Italian favorite, not quite a salsa, but definitely a flavor booster. Use this whenever chopped parsley does not seem like enough. For the freshest flavor, use within an hour or two. Combine ingredients.

Herbed Cheese:
Combine cream cheese, chèvre, shallot and clove of garlic, dill, chives, parsley, add ¼ t ground pepper and salt. Mix well and let stand at least one hour. This improves overnight.

Meringue:
This is another "Little Black Dress" for the kitchen. It makes individual shells, a large one for Pavlova, and small kisses.
For 10-12 individual shells or 1 large shell: whip egg whites in a non plastic bowl until very soft peaks form, gradually add sugar mixed with cornstarch and beat until stiff and glossy, but not dry. Add lemon juice and vanilla. On a baking sheet lined with parchment or foil, make 2-3 inch circles with a piping bag or 1 large circle 9 inches in diameter. Bake at 250˚ for 1 hour, for the small shells, 1 ¼ hours for the Pavlova, rotating pans halfway through. Turn off heat and let sit in oven for another hour.
You may also make about 40 bite size kisses with the meringue. If you do not have a piping bag, a big baggie with ½ inch cut off the corner works also. The meringues will keep in an air tight container for 2 weeks as long as it is not humid.

1 cut up stick unsalted butter
½ cup whole milk
½ cup water
½ t salt
1 cup flour
4 large room temperature eggs

Pâte á Choux:

You will amaze yourself and your friends with this invaluable recipe. It makes so many delicious things such as Profiteroles, Cream Puffs, Beignets, Gourgeres, and Éclairs. Best of all, in a pinch, the dough can keep for 2 days in a pastry bag in the refrigerator. Place the pastry bag in a zip lock baggie.

In a saucepan over medium heat, put butter, milk, water, salt, and bring to a boil stirring until the butter is melted. Take off the heat. Immediately pour flour into the pan and stir vigorously. A wooden spoon works best here. When the dough is smooth, return to the heat. Continue to cook until there are no lumps and the dough pulls away from the pan. About 1 minute. Remove from the heat and drop the dough into a food processor fitted with the metal blade; let cool slightly then add eggs 1 at a time. The dough will be shiny and stiff. Do not work it too hard. It is now ready to make into fabulous bites.

Cream Puffs:

Put the dough in a pastry bag and depending on the size you want, pipe the dough onto a baking sheet covered with parchment or silicone baking mat. Make 1 ½ inch mounds 2 inches apart. With a wet finger tamp down the pointy tips. Bake in a 400˚ oven for 5 minutes. Reduce heat to 350˚ and bake 10 minutes longer. Turn off the oven and with the door closed let them sit for 20 minutes to get crisp. This recipe will make 36 small puffs or 12-16 large ones.

Gourgeres: (pictured on page 37)

Add 1 cup coarsely grated or diced Gruyere cheese and freshly ground pepper. For cocktail parties I like to make these small so that they are just one perfect bite. Cook for 15 minutes until golden. For a party table they look very festive made into larger balls and cooked in a ring. For the ring they will need to cook for 20 minutes. They may be reheated in a 325˚ oven for 10 minutes.

1 lb. pecans
3 T butter
3 t Worcestershire sauce
1 t salt
½ t cinnamon
¼ t cumin
¼ t cayenne
¼ t Tabasco sauce
½ cup turbinado sugar

1 cup water
1½ cup sugar

Salad Dressings

3 egg yolks
3 T lemon juice
½ cup each chopped:
tarragon and chervil
1 cup chopped parsley
6 chopped green onions
2 oz. can flat anchovies
1 cup extra virgin olive oil

½ cup olive oil
juice of 1 lime
1 T honey
salt and pepper

½ cup olive oil
2 T vinegar
salt
pepper freshly ground

Spicy Pecans:
I usually double this recipe as these nuts do not stay around long. You definitely cannot eat just one. These make excellent hostess gifts.
In a large frying pan put butter, Worcestershire, salt, cinnamon, cumin, cayenne, Tabasco and sugar. Cook until it starts to thicken and sugar is melted; then add 1 lb. pecans. Stir well. Pour into a baking pan, spread out into one layer and bake in a 325˚ oven for 15-20 minutes stirring every 5 minutes. They tend to get a little clumpy. You have to pay attention when you make these as they burn easily.

Simple Syrup:
Simmer water and sugar to completely dissolve sugar. Cool. This makes about 1 ½ cups, and keeps for a couple of days.

Green Goddess Dressing:
I love this dressing, but if you are worried about raw eggs substitute 1 cup good mayonnaise for the egg yolks and olive oil.
Purée first seven ingredients in a blender and then very slowly add 1 cup oil. It will keep for one week in the refrigerator. If you want it really green add 2 cups baby spinach in the blender just before serving.

Honey Lime Dressing:
You can make Honey-Mustard Dressing by adding 1 T Dijon mustard or add 2 T chopped mint to the oil, honey and lime for a Lime Mint Dressing.

Simple Vinaigrette:
Use any vinegar such as red wine, white wine, balsamic, rice etc. You may also add a pinch of herbs.

Vinaigrette:
For Vinaigrette use recipe for Simple Vinaigrette and add 1 T Dijon mustard.

½ cup buttermilk
½ cup light sour cream
½ cup mayonnaise
2 T each parsley and chives
1 clove minced garlic
2 t lime juice
pepper

Ranch Dressing:
Blend. This keeps several days.

Sauces

1 large chopped onion
3 T olive oil
1 28 oz. can San Marzano
Tomato Purée
3 T chopped basil

Basil/Tomato Sauce:
For this basic sauce it is important to use San Marzano Tomato Purée. Sauté onion in olive oil until caramelized. Add tomatoes. Simmer for 30 minutes. This will keep for a week, but add the fresh basil the day you use the sauce.

1 full cup of dried mushrooms
such as porcini
hot water to cover about 1½ cups
1 onion grated
½ cup water
2 T butter
2 T olive oil
2 cloves minced garlic
1 T meat extract
salt and pepper

Babalu Sauce:
Take the dried mushrooms and soak in hot water to cover for 1 hour. Reserving the liquid, when soft, chop mushrooms fairly finely. Meanwhile, sauté onion in butter and olive oil, add garlic. Add the chopped mushrooms and the strained liquid to the sauce, add ½ cup water. Simmer for 30 minutes; do not let boil. At this point add your meat extract. Salt and pepper to taste. The sauce will hold for a couple of days.

Consie's Shrimp Frittata

2

BRUNCHES

Sunday Brunch

Summer Frittata

Norwegian Breakfast

Family Buffet Brunch

Brunches have to be the easiest party for the cook to give. The time is flexible, there are no courses, and usually only one other beverage is offered besides coffee. I find you can prepare most of the meal the day before. The best thing is that most people are in a relaxed mode and ready to have fun.

Sunday Brunch

For 10

This is a very easy on the cook brunch. The crèpes may be made days before and the filling the night before. Have people nibble on the fish as you sip a mimosa and sauté the blintzes.

Mimosas
Smoked Fish with Rye Crackers
Blintzes with Fruit
Chicken Apple Sausages
Café au Lait

2 bottles sparkling wine
½ gallon of orange/
tangerine juice
10 small berries

Mimosas:
Put a berry in the bottom of 10 Champagne flutes; fill glasses 2/3 full of sparkling wine and top with juice.

1¼ lbs. smoked fish
1 thinly sliced European cucumber
1 thinly sliced lemon

Smoked Fish:
Place your fish of choice on a platter with rye crackers or cocktail rye bread and slices of cucumber and lemon.

Blintzes with Fruit

20 crèpes* see Basics
1 lb. ricotta
1T grated lemon peel
2 t cinnamon
1 t nutmeg
3 t sugar
1 stick butter
½ cup turbinado sugar
Cinnamon Sugar

Blintzes:
Fill 20 crèpes* with ricotta that has been mixed with lemon peel, nutmeg, cinnamon and sugar. Roll up with closed ends making a neat package; do this before your guests arrive.

Melt butter and sugar in a sauté pan and sauté blintzes until golden. Place on plate and sprinkle with cinnamon sugar. Serve hot.

2 T cinnamon
1 cup sugar

Cinnamon Sugar:
Mix together and store in a dry place.

1-2 chicken apple sausages per person

Apple Chicken Sausages:
Before guests arrive cook sausages in a frying pan for 10-15 minutes turning often. Keep warm in the 250˚ oven.

5 bananas sliced
2 cups sour cream
1 pint seasonal berries

To serve: Mix the bananas with 1 cup of the sour cream. On each plate place sausages, 2 blintzes, and some bananas and top with remaining sour cream and berries.

per drink:
¾ cup strong coffee, such as French Roast
½ cup scalded milk

Café au Lait:
Café au Lait is not a latte! In New Orleans, the coffee is always made with part chicory which adds a very different flavor. The French frequently drink their morning Café au Lait in bowls so large you have to surround it with two hands. All the better to inhale the delicious aroma.

Summer Frittata

For 12

This brunch calls out for bright colors in the flowers and the place settings.

Joyful Sunrises
Prosciutto and Melon
Consie's Shrimp Frittata
with Guacamole
Sourdough Toast with Fresh Nectarine
Jam

Per drink
2 oz. tequila
4 oz. orange/tangerine juice
½ oz. pomegranate concentrate

Joyful Sunrise:

Fill a tall glass with ice cubes. Pour in tequila and juice, stir. Tip the glass and pour the concentrate down the side of the glass. Pomegranate juice is VERY healthy, full of antioxidants, and no extra sugar! Garnish with a slice of orange.

Joyful Sunrises

2 melons
1 lb. thinly sliced prosciutto
2 limes

Prosciutto and Melon:

Cut the sweetest melons available into 12 wedges. Remove the seeds and the rind. Drape pieces of prosciutto over the melon. Serve with lime wedges.

Frittata:

1 lb. peeled and coarsely chopped shrimp
2 cloves minced garlic
3 T butter
20 large eggs
2 cups grated pepper jack cheese

Consie's Shrimp Frittata: (pictured on page 18)
Our wonderful daughter-in-law Consie made this up.
In a non stick pan sauté shrimp in chopped garlic and butter for about 2 minutes until shrimp are JUST pink.

Whip eggs and add to the shrimp. Stir until almost set then add the cheese. Put the heat on low and cook covered for 2-3 minutes, until the cheese is melted. Let sit 3 minutes. You may have to do this in 2 pans. If you only have 1 pan, put the first frittata in some heavy foil and keep warm in a 275° oven. It does hold quite well.

2 large avocados peeled
1 large tomato
½ cup chopped cilantro
1 lime juiced
Cholula Hot Sauce*

Guacamole:
Avocados should be **slightly** soft to the touch, not hard, not mushy. Mash with a fork. Add a peeled and chopped tomato, cilantro, lime juice, salt, and Cholula as you like for heat.

To serve: cut the frittata into wedges and put a dollop of guacamole on top of each piece.

1 loaf sourdough bread

Toast bread slices.

5 large chopped and pitted nectarines
2/3 cup sugar
1 lemon

Nectarine Jam:
In a small sauce pan put sugar and the juice of ½ a lemon; melt the sugar in the juice and then add the chopped nectarines. Simmer on low until the jam is very thick, stirring often. This jam should have almost no liquid. It will keep for 3 weeks in the refrigerator. This recipe works equally well with 12 large figs.

Fish:
Gravlax (recipe follows)
16 oz. pickled herring in sour cream
2 cans sardines

1 package of each:
pumpernickel bread
flat bread
Rye Crisp crackers
cracked wheat bread

½ lb. piece of each cheese:
Jarlsberg
Havarti
Gouda

Meat:
½ lb. sliced ham
½ lb. sliced salami
8 oz. liverwurst

Eggs:
1 ½ dozen hard boiled

Condiments:
lingonberry jelly
1 sliced European cucumber
8 small tomatoes sliced
sliced lemon

Rosettes (recipe follows)

Norwegian Breakfast
For 16

We spent a lot of time in Norway and the breakfasts were the favorite meal. Now I always have to make this menu when we are all together. There are a lot of items but not much last minute cooking, so this is an excellent way to spend a long Sunday morning. In the hotels in Norway the food goes on forever, with so many varieties of cheese and meats and breads and fish and cereals you can't choose. They do not put every thing on one plate; you start with the fish, and then get other plates for the rest. You can find many of these items at IKEA or a Scandinavian store.

Gravlax

This meal is best served buffet style. All like items are placed together; all the breads in a flat basket, the eggs in a bowl, and the herring in a bowl. Place the meats and cheese on a platter with the sliced tomatoes. Artfully presented, this makes an impressive display with very little work.

4 lbs. center cut salmon
½ cup kosher salt
6 T sugar
3 T ground pepper
1 small bunch dill

For the Gravlax:
The salmon is cured with salt and sugar. This is such a family favorite that I have had to make it for 100s at the kid's weddings! Make this and everyone will think you are a "culinary genius". I have made this so often that it now takes me ten minutes to make.

At least **2 days before**, (preferably 3) take the salmon filet with the skin on, and cut it in half. If you have to buy the whole filet, trim the small ends and the top off so that you will have pieces of equal thickness. Mix non-iodized kosher salt and sugar with freshly ground pepper. On 2 pieces of heavy duty foil spread 1/3 of the sugar/salt mixture, put one piece of the salmon skin-side down, put another third of the mixture on the flesh side, and add a small bunch of chopped dill. Top with the other piece of salmon, fitting the pieces together and put the rest of the salt mix on top. Make a "box" of the foil by bringing up the sides of the foil, and fold the top. You will have a package that should keep the resulting brine from spilling out. It is a good idea to put it on a jelly roll pan. Refrigerate. After 12 hours, open the package and turn over the salmon as one piece. Close back up. Let sit in the refrigerator an additional 24 hours. At this point, turn once more, and leave for 12 more hours. It is now ready, but will keep for several days. Remove the salmon from the marinade, pat dry and wrap in plastic wrap. To serve, slice thinly at a slant (you need a very sharp knife for this) leaving the skin behind. Serve with lemon, and the rest of the fixings. If there is any leftover salmon wrap it in plastic wrap. This does freeze but the texture is different, so it is good to add to scrambled eggs, in a hors d'oeuvre roll, or mixed with pasta.

2 eggs beaten
2 T sugar
1 cup milk
1 cup sifted flour
½ t salt
1 t lemon extract
powdered sugar

Rosettes:

A fun interactive ending are fried cookies made with a special Scandinavian tool called a Rosette Iron.

Heat 1 quart of canola oil to 365˚.

Mix all ingredients together to form a batter. Take the cookie iron and plunge into the hot oil and then dip into the batter and then back in the oil. It is ready when bubbling ceases and the cookie is golden. Be sure that you do not let the batter overrun the top of the iron. If you do, it is almost impossible to remove the cookie in one piece. Sprinkle with a little powdered sugar. Yum! Light, crispy and not too sweet.

Rosettes

Family Buffet Brunch
For 8-10
This is a very family friendly menu and is easily doubled.

Orange Smiles

Never Fail Soufflé

Ham

Gouda

Walnut and Apple Crisp

6 unpeeled washed navel
oranges

Orange Smiles:
Cut each orange into 8 wedges.

Orange Smiles

1 loaf firm white bread
2 ½ cups sharp cheese
grated
1 dozen eggs
1 ½ cups half and half
1 cup milk
salt and pepper
pinch red pepper flakes
6 T melted butter

Never Fail Soufflé:
We make this easy on the cook soufflé every Christmas morning.

Remove crust from bread and cut the bread into 1 inch cubes. In a bowl beat eggs with half and half, milk, salt and pepper to taste and a pinch of red pepper flakes. Add the grated cheese to the mixture. In a buttered 9 x13 baking pan, spread out bread cubes in the pan and pour mixture over bread. Let sit covered in the refrigerator overnight. Right before baking, drizzle with melted butter. Bake for 45 minutes at 350˚.

Variation:
To make the soufflé a little spicier, I frequently add 1 small can chopped

(previous soufflé recipe)
1 4 oz. can chopped green peppers
1 lb. bulk sausage

4 lb. pre-cooked ham
½ cup brown sugar
¼ cup Dijon Mustard
1 lb. wedge Gouda cheese
large package of grapes

2 cups walnuts or pecan pieces or combination
3 lbs. Granny Smith apples
3 lbs. Macintosh apples
1 t ground cloves
½ stick butter

½ t nutmeg
2 t cinnamon
1 cup dark brown sugar
1½ cups flour
1 cup rolled oats (not instant)
1 stick butter

green peppers to the cheese. You may also add 1 lb. bulk sausage that has been browned; make layers of bread and sausage reduce cheese to 1 cup, and use ½ the cheese as a topping.

Ham: Bake ham with a glaze made of ½ cup brown sugar, and ¼ cup Dijon mustard. Bake the ham at 300˚ for ½ hour for precooked hams. Slice the ham and place on a large platter with a large wedge of Gouda. Decorate with bunches of grapes. Little kids love grapes.

Alternatively have a platter of sliced deli ham.

Walnut and Apple Crisp:
Toast nut pieces in a 375˚ oven for 5 minutes, watching that they do not burn.
Peel, core and quarter the apples to make 8 cups. Butter a 9 x13 baking dish and put in the apples; sprinkle with the ground cloves and dot with bits of butter.

Topping:
In the processor put the nutmeg, cinnamon, sugar, flour, oats, and mix with cold butter cut into 1 T pieces. Process quickly. Spread topping over the apples and sprinkle nuts on top. Bake at 375˚ for 55 minutes. If you make this the day before, cook for 40 minutes and on the morning reheat for 15 minutes to warm. This will serve 10 or 12 if served with ice cream as a dessert.

Rocky Road Ice Cream Sandwiches

3

LUNCHEONS

Spring Buffet

A Guy's Lunch

Autumn Luncheon

Holiday Vegetarian Luncheon

Luncheons may be elegant or casual depending on you and your guests. Because there are no cocktails and appetizers, if you need to adhere to a strict time frame luncheons work very well.

Spring Buffet Luncheon

For 12

Pots of primroses look springy fresh as centerpieces. Echo their colors in your table cloth.

Gewürztraminer
Sparkling Pomegranate Juice
Fresh Hearts of Palm
with
Shrimp Salad
Middle East Salad
Cilantro Chicken Salad
A Basket of Gougeres*
Curry Crackers
Pistachio Dream

Gewürztraminer is a dry fruity white wine that pairs well with the various spices in this meal.

3 6 inch sections fresh palm hearts

Fresh Hearts of Palm Salad:
Two Weeks ahead on the internet, order from "DeKing of Hearts" 3 6-inch sections of hearts of palm. Slice the palm hearts thinly. You may use canned hearts but the taste is not the same.

2½ lbs. small salad shrimp
1 T fresh basil chopped
1 T guava jelly
½ cup minced sweet onion
pinch of pepper flakes
4 T olive oil
3 T lemon juice
1 head of frisée lettuce
3 fresh guavas

Shrimp Salad:
If the shrimp are uncooked, place in boiling water until they are just pink, about 1-2 minutes. Drain. Mix with basil, guava jelly, sweet onion, pepper flakes and oil. You may mix this the day before.

Just before serving mix shrimp with lemon juice. On a platter, put the shrimp in the middle then surround with the slices of palm. Garnish the platter with frisée and wedges of fresh guava. If you can not find fresh guavas, use 3 peeled and sliced kiwis.

1 cup chopped mint
1 cup chopped parsley
2 European chopped cucumbers
2 large tomatoes chopped
1 finely minced sweet onion
1 finely minced clove garlic
juice of a lemon
2½ T olive oil

Middle East Salad:
Mix all the salad ingredients together. The salad can sit for 4 hours. If you make it the day before, it is still good but not as fresh and crunchy. You can chop everything the day before and put in individual containers, then mix that day.

2 heads Bibb lettuce

Keeping the largest outer leaves and the smallest inner leaves for garnishing the platter, place portions of the salad in the medium leaves and arrange on a platter. You may prep the greens the day before and put into a baggie.

1 cup crumbled feta
1 cup chopped kalamata olives

Garnish:
Garnish with the olives and feta scattered over the salad.

2½ lbs. breasts of chicken
½ cup mayonnaise
1 red onion minced
3 T rice vinegar
4 ribs celery chopped
2 bunches of red seedless grapes
1 bunch cilantro
Champagne grapes

Cilantro Chicken Salad:
Cut whole breasts of chicken in half and cook in a covered pan of simmering water to cover for 15 minutes. Let cool in the water for 30-40 minutes then cut into bite size pieces and mix with mayonnaise, red onion, vinegar, celery, 2 cups grapes and 1 cup cilantro leaves. May be made the day before without the cilantro and grapes; add them at the last minute. The chicken may be cooked 2 days before; refrigerate. Embellish the platter with grape bunches, use "Champagne Grapes" if you can find them, and cilantro sprigs.

1½ cups flour
½ t baking powder
¼ t salt
2 t curry powder
cayenne
6 T soft butter
1 egg
2 t tomato paste

Curry Crackers:
Prepare several baking sheets with buttered parchment or silicone baking mat. Preheat oven to 400˚.
Mix in the food processor, flour, baking powder, salt, curry powder, dash of cayenne, butter until fine crumbs form. In a small bowl beat egg with tomato paste, add to the flour and mix well until smooth. On a floured surface, roll out the dough into 1/8th inch thickness; cut into about 30 3 x 1¾ triangles or use cookie cutters. Re-work, roll out and cut until all the dough is used.
Bake for 12-14 minutes until lightly browned. These will keep in an airtight container for several days.

1 recipe Gourgeres*
See Basics

Basket of Gourgeres

1½ cups shelled pistachios,
divided
½ cup sugar
6 egg whites
¼ cup sugar
2 cups whipping cream
¼ t vanilla
top quality chocolate sauce
1 cup chopped pistachios

Pistachio Dream:
Pulse in a food processor 1 cup shelled pistachios with the ½ cup sugar
until finely ground. Add ½ cup more nuts and pulse just until very
coarsely ground. You want some bits of pistachio. In a mixer, beat egg
whites until soft peaks form then add ¼ cup sugar; beat until stiff peaks
form. Do not over beat, as the whites will dry out. In another bowl whip
cream with vanilla. Fold together and put into 12 freezer proof bowls,
like small ramekins. Or freeze in a long loaf pan lined with plastic wrap,
unmold to serve in slices. Freeze 6 hours or overnight. Defrost 30
minutes before serving. Serve drizzled with chocolate sauce and sprinkle
more pistachios on top.

A Guy's Lunch
For 4
Your favorite guy will love this lunch.
A red checkered tablecloth with clay
pots of herbs seems appropriate.

Beer
Cold Potato Soup
Bread Sticks
Steak Salad
Bean salad
Rocky Road Ice Cream Sandwiches

2 T butter
1 large chopped onion
2 large peeled and chopped
Russet potatoes
2 cups milk
Cholula Sauce
chives

Cold Potato Soup:
Sauté onion in butter until opaque; add potatoes, salt and pepper and water to cover. Simmer until potatoes are fork tender. In a blender, put vegetables, and milk. Blend and chill; just before serving add juice of ½ a lemon and dash of Cholula.
Serve cold with snipped chives.

1½ lbs. thick top sirloin steak
or 1 ½ lbs. flank steak
1 Walla Walla or Vidallia
onion
4 T balsamic vinegar
4 strips thick cut bacon
½ lb. baby spinach
4 T sour cream
1 T horseradish
8 cherry tomatoes

Steak Salad:
First, in a bowl put onion that has been cut into thin slices, and pour the balsamic vinegar over them. Mix well.
Grill the steak over medium heat, 7 minutes on a side. The inside temperature should be 125˚. Fry bacon until crisp. These 3 items may be done in the morning and refrigerated. Take spinach and divide between 4 plates. Slice steaks into strips and fan out on top of the spinach. If you use flank steak cut on the diagonal. Divide onion among the plates topping the steak. Combine sour cream and horseradish and drizzle over the salad. Crumble one piece of bacon on each salad, and salt and pepper to taste. Garnish with a couple of halved cherry tomatoes per plate. Serve with the bean salad and bread sticks.

2 cups cooked cannellini beans
3 stalks chopped celery
1 lime
2 T olive oil
salt and pepper

Bean Salad:
Mix the cannellini beans with the celery, lime juice, salt, pepper, and oil. May be made the day before.

1 pint Rocky Road Ice Cream
or
1 pint chocolate ice cream
1 cup marshmallow fluff
16 chocolate chip cookies

Rocky Road Ice Cream Sandwiches: (pictured on page 32)
Make your favorite chocolate chip cookies in a 3 inch size.
If Rocky Road ice cream is unavailable, you can make your own. Simply mix fluff with slightly softened ice cream.
Spread slightly softened ice cream between 2 cookies. Allow 2 sandwiches per person. Individually wrap the cookie sandwich in plastic wrap and freeze. These need to be made at least 4 hours before, and will keep frozen, individually wrapped for a week.

Autumn Luncheon

For 6

A centerpiece of curly cabbages and green apples would be lovely. A few open white roses will add panache.

Sparkling Water   Viognier

Mini Popovers

Watercress and Apple Soup

Duck Salad

Wild Rice Salad

Bumble's Ginger Roll

Viognier is a fragrant and rich white wine now made in California.

4 extra large eggs
2 cups flour
2 cups milk
2 T melted butter
salt
16 t vegetable oil for regular size muffins
or
oil spray for the mini size

Mini Popovers:
Lightly beat 4 extra large eggs; set aside. Whisk together sifted flour, milk, butter, pinch salt, and when mixed, add in the eggs. It should look like very heavy cream. Let sit one hour. The batter will hold covered and refrigerated overnight. Bring to room temperature and stir well. Have ready a 450° oven. Heat heavy muffin tin, place 1 t oil in each cup and fill half full with batter. Bake for 15 minutes and then turn down oven to 350°. Do not peek! Cook for another 20 minutes until dark golden brown. This makes 12-16 regular muffin size popovers; for mini popovers use **heavy** mini muffin tins to cook, decreasing the oil to a drop and the cooking time to about 20 minutes.

2 large leeks
2 T butter
1 quart homemade chicken broth
2 Granny Smith apples
1 small Russet potato
1 bunch watercress

Watercress and Apple Soup:
In a large sauce pan, sauté chopped, well washed leeks, white part only, in butter; add broth, peeled and chopped apples, peeled and chopped potato, and cook until apple and potato are soft. The soup may be made to here a day ahead.

Reserving 6 sprigs for garnish, add 1 bunch chopped watercress to the boiling soup base. Cook for a couple of minutes until watercress is slightly cooked. You want the cress to still have a fresh green look. Pour into a blender in two batches until well blended. Serve hot or cold with a sprig of watercress for garnish.

1 Napa cabbage

Napa Cabbage:
Wash and slice the cabbage into ½ inch strips. This is the bed for the duck. Savoy cabbage will work here as well.

8 oz. fresh cranberries
1 unpeeled navel orange
½ cup sugar

Cranberry/Orange Relish: Place all in the processor and chop. It needs to be slightly chunky. This will keep for 4-5 days but is best the first 2 days.

Duck Breast Salad

2 whole Muscovy duck breasts (about 3 lbs. total)

½ cup honey
1 T light soy sauce
1 T Chinese 5 Spice

5 T chopped red onion
1 cup cranberry/orange relish
1 cup cranberries
1 orange zested

Honey Glazed Duck Breast Salad:
Using a very sharp knife, score the fat side of the duck breasts in a cross hatch pattern, making sure not to cut into the flesh. Heat the oven to 210˚. Sear the breasts, fat side down in a medium hot frying pan until the skin is crisp, about 7 minutes, turn over, and cook other side for 5 minutes until meat is medium rare.

Glaze:
Remove breast from pan and place in oven proof dish. Glaze breasts with a mix of honey, soy sauce and Chinese 5 Spice, then place in warm oven.

Sauce:
In the same frying pan, using 2 T of the duck fat, sauté the onion. Then add 1 cup of relish and cook 3 minutes. Add any leftover glaze to the sauce.

To serve: Remove duck from the oven and slice into strips. Place a handful of cabbage on each plate and divide the hot duck, fanning out the slices. Pour some sauce on each serving. Garnish with whole cranberries and zest.

1 cup wild rice
2 green onions chopped
½ cup yellow raisins chopped
½ cup cashews chopped
Asian Dressing (below)

Asian Dressing:

¼ cup sesame seed oil
2 T rice vinegar
1 t light soy sauce
hot pepper sauce to taste

Wild Rice Salad:

Cook rinsed wild rice in 3 cups water. Bring to a boil and then reduce heat to a simmer. Cook for about 40 minutes. It should still have a "bite", and most of the moisture will have been absorbed. May be cooked to here 1 day ahead. Cool. Toss together. May be made early in the morning. Serve alongside the duck.

6 T unsalted butter
½ cup plus 1 T light molasses
¼ cup turbinado sugar
½ cup water
1 large egg divided
1 cup cake flour
½ t baking powder
1 T ground ginger
1 cup whipping cream
¼ cup white sugar
½ cup finely chopped crystallized ginger
½ cup powdered sugar for sifting

Bumbles Ginger Roll:

This is my American adaptation of a famous dessert from Bumbles Restaurant in London, England. The filled cake may be made 1 day in advance and refrigerated.

Put parchment in a jelly roll pan and butter. Preheat oven to 350˚. Melt butter, molasses, sugar, and water in a sauce pan. Cool stirring frequently. When cool add the egg yolk. Mix cake flour with baking powder and ginger and sift. Add to the butter mixture, mix well. Beat the white of 1 egg until stiff. Fold the egg white into the batter, and then pour into the prepared pan. Bake for 15 minutes, let cool 5 minutes then turn out the cake onto a clean tea towel, not on a terry cloth towel. Take off the parchment paper. If any bits come off, no one will know for it will be covered with cream.

Whip the cream with the sugar and spread filling on the cake. Roll up using the towel as an aid. Can be refrigerated here for a day. Sift powdered sugar over the cake. Slice with a serrated knife. Sprinkle each slice with chopped ginger.

Holiday
Vegetarian Luncheon

For 12

Vegetarian or not, you will love this menu. This is a very pretty red and green meal. Evergreens with the addition of 3 red blooming Amaryllis marching down the table would be a lovely centerpiece. Have everyone bring cookies to trade.

Fume Blanc
Red Pepper Soup
Cheese Straws
Eggplant Stacks
Frisée Salad with Roasted Pears
Holiday Cookies

Fume Blanc is a white wine delicious with this menu.

4 T olive oil
4 cups chopped onions
4 cloves minced garlic
10 chopped red peppers
4 topped, peeled and
chopped carrots
8 cups vegetable broth
2 t smoked paprika
salt and pepper
1 lemon
1 cup heavy cream
chives

Red Pepper Soup:
Try to use carrots that come with tops for this soup. They have a much better flavor.
In a large sauce pan sauté the onions in the oil until transparent, add the garlic and cook 2 minutes; then add the chopped vegetables and the broth. Simmer until the carrots are tender. Salt and pepper to taste. Purée the soup in a blender in 2 batches or with an immersion blender. Strain. If the soup seems too thick, add more broth. The soup may be made to here 1 day ahead. Just before serving, bring the soup back to a simmer and add in the juice of the lemon. Drizzle a tablespoon of the cream on top of each bowl of soup in a nice pattern. Snip some chives on top.

Red Pepper Soup

½ package frozen puff pastry
1 egg white
1¼ cup grated parmesan cheese
dash cayenne pepper

Cheese Straws:

Yet another great application for frozen puff pastry. Roll out ½ of the package of the dough. Brush the pastry with egg white that has been beaten with the parmesan cheese and cayenne. Cut into 6 x 1 inch lengths. Twist lengths into spirals. Place on a parchment covered sheet and bake for 10 minutes at 400˚. These may be made 2-3 days ahead, placed in an air tight container and reheated for 3 minutes.

2 large eggplants
9 T olive oil
2 diced onions
4 cloves minced garlic
2 small diced green peppers
2 14.5 oz. cans diced tomatoes
2 cans of water
2 rounds of fresh buffalo mozzarella sliced
12 sprigs fresh basil
2 cups dry bread crumbs

Eggplant Stacks:

Pre-heat the oven to 375˚.
Peel and slice the eggplant into ½ inch thick slices. You will need 24 slices. Place the slices in a colander and liberally salt the slices. Let sit 45 minutes.

Meanwhile, make a sauce of the diced onion, garlic and peppers by sautéing them in 3 T of the oil. When onion is opaque, add the tomatoes and 2 cans of water. Cook for about 10 minutes. The sauce may be made the day before.

Rinse and pat dry eggplant and place the eggplant in a flat baking dish and drizzle with the rest of the oil. Bake for 15 minutes. Remove. Slice the cheese into 12 thick slices; 6 slices per round.

In a baking dish, put 1/3 of the sauce. Make 12 stacks by putting a slice of eggplant, a slice of mozzarella, another slice of eggplant. You may need to place the smaller slices of eggplant on the tops. Place the stacks on top of the sauce and then spoon another 1/3 sauce on top of the stacks keeping the remaining for presentation. Put a bit of the crumbs on top of each stack, using it all. The stacks may be held here for a couple of hours. Bake for 20 minutes, heating the stacks so that the cheese is melting and the crumbs crispy.

24 large 1½-2 inch
mushroom caps
3 T butter
1 T Oregon white truffle oil

Cut the stems from the mushrooms. Sauté the mushroom caps in the butter. May be done ahead and reheated. Just before serving drizzle the truffle oil over the mushrooms.

To serve: Heat the remaining sauce and put some on each plate; add a stack, 2 mushrooms and a piece of fresh basil.

olive oil
sea salt
6 Bosc pears

Roasted Pears:
Preheat oven to 300˚.
Core the pears, and then slice into 8ths. Have a baking pan brushed with olive oil ready. Place the sliced pears in one layer, and salt with freshly ground sea salt. Bake for 1 hour or until the pear slices have lost most of their moisture. The pears will keep in an airtight container in the refrigerator for 2 days.

2 bunches of frisée
1 cup Spicy Pecans*
Camberzola cheese (optional)
Balsamic Vinaigrette* See
Basics

Frisée Salad with Roasted Pears:
Arrange the frisée on 12 salad plates and then put the pears on top. Dress with Vinaigrette.* Sprinkle the pecans on top. This salad is delicious with a slice of Camberzola cheese.

Holiday cookies for dessert

Holiday Cookies:
I love holiday cookie exchanges, especially if everyone makes them from old family recipes. Some of my favorite holiday cookie recipes come from exchanges. Have everyone bring 11 copies of the recipe as well as the cookies. Hope you get some delicious treats!

Grilled Jerk Chicken with Corn and Red Pepper Jubilee

4

PICNICS

Spring Barbeque

Summer Boat Party

Fall Barbeque

Fireside Dinner

Picnics may be at home or away. To me, it just means that it is not the "same old same old". We all need to put a little variety in our lives and have fun.

Spring Barbeque

For 8

Some of us can hardly wait for the first BBQ, whether it is at home or at another site. This BBQ easily may be doubled for a larger crowd.

Margaritas
Bacon Wrapped Scallops
Cabernet
Grilled Steaks
Italian Salsa Verde
Grilled Vegetables
Confetti Slaw
The BEST Corn Bread
Berries and Cookies or Sorbet and Kisses*

Per drink
3 oz Tequila
2 oz. Cointreau
1 oz fresh lime juice
1 cup crushed ice
1 slice lime

Margaritas:

Pour into a shaker, or blender if making a large batch, until ice cold. Pour into a salt rimmed glass and decorate with a slice of lime. If your BBQ is away from home premix the Margaritas without the ice.

1 dozen large dry scallops
1 1 lb. package thinly sliced bacon
½ cup Hoisin Sauce
2 T rice vinegar

Bacon Wrapped Scallops:

Slice the scallops in half. Cut bacon strips in half and wrap around the scallops and secure with a toothpick. Mix sauce and vinegar and brush on each scallop. Reserve remainder of sauce for dipping. Grill in a grill basket turning to cook bacon. If you are BBQing at home you may bake the scallops in a 375° oven for about 10 minutes until bacon is cooked. These may be prepared ahead and frozen. Just be sure that they are well defrosted before you cook them. This recipe makes 3 per person which seems like a lot, but they go fast.

4 anchovies
2 hard boiled egg yolks
1 packed cup parsley
2 cloves garlic
6 T olive oil
4 T lemon juice

Italian Salsa Verde:

Dan's Italian Grandmother made this without a blender. I love blenders! Use the small jar unless you double this recipe which I usually do as it is so tasty on toast. Do not be put off by the anchovy it just acts as salt. Really. Make sure your capers are the small ones as the large ones will not work here.

Separate the yolks from the whites and reserve whites for the Meringue Kisses*. Cook the yolks in simmering water until hard.
In a blender put anchovies, egg yolks, parsley, garlic, olive oil, and lemon juice.

1 t freshly ground pepper
2 T rinsed small capers

Pulse quickly so as not to make a paste, and remove from the blender; add pepper and the capers.

Cabernet: A great red wine for this meal.

8 4-6 oz. steaks
(rib eye works great here)
salt and pepper to taste

2 thickly sliced sweet onions
1 lb. trimmed baby carrots
2 lbs. trimmed asparagus cut
into 3 in. pieces
1 lemon
salt and pepper

1 diced red pepper
1 diced yellow pepper
½ red onion diced
bunch of cilantro
1 thinly sliced Napa cabbage
1 T sugar
2 T rice vinegar
salt and pepper
3 T olive oil

Grilled Steaks:
Liberally salt and pepper the steaks and grill over a medium hot flame about 5 minutes per side for rare. Serve the meat with a dollop of salsa.

Grilled Vegetables:
On a grill pan put the onion with the carrots; grill stirring often until just done, about 10-15 minutes. Add the asparagus for about 3 minutes. Remove to a platter and sprinkle the juice of a lemon over the vegetables. If you do not want to cook these at the picnic site, stir fry at home in 1T olive oil. Salt and pepper to taste. Serve at room temperature.

Confetti Slaw:
Add ¾ of a bunch of cilantro stemmed and chopped to the peppers, onion, and cabbage. You may prep the vegetables the day before and place in separate baggies. Make a dressing of sugar, vinegar, oil, salt and pepper and toss with the veggies. Put sprigs of cilantro on top.

Confetti Slaw

3 cups cornmeal
1 cup flour
1 t baking powder
1 t baking soda
2 t salt
2 lightly beaten large eggs
2 T honey
3 cups buttermilk
3 sticks unsalted butter, divided and melted

The BEST Corn Bread:

The corn bread is best warm, but you may assemble the dry ingredients several days ahead. This makes terrific bread for stuffing a bird.

This makes 2 skillet breads baked in 10" iron skillets that have been heated in a 425˚ oven. If you do not have the skillets, use a large 9 x13 pan. The bread will not be as crispy, but it is still good.

Mix dry ingredients, add milk, eggs, honey and 1 cup butter. Divide remaining ½ cup butter between the two hot pans. Pour half of the batter in each pan. Bake for 10 minutes and then switch position of the pans in the oven. Cook for 10 more minutes, until a toothpick in the middle comes out clean. If you are using the large pan, put ½ cup butter in it, add batter and bake for 30-35 minutes.

8 cups puréed berries
3 T lemon juice
1 cup Simple Syrup *

Berries or Sorbet:

If you are away from home bring a basket of the first strawberries and cookies, or if home make a strawberry sorbet and kisses.

Sorbet:

I love sorbets and you can make them without a machine. They taste delicious and are easy to prepare. Try various flavors of simple syrup, infuse with herbs such as mint or basil.

Place fruit in a blender with lemon juice and syrup. Blend well. Put the fruit purée into individual ramekins and freeze for at least 6 hours. Garnish with a basil or mint leaf.

Kisses*: See Basics under Meringues

Summer Boat Party

For 6

Be sure to have BIG napkins for this dinner. Whenever I find fun tea towels I use them for picnic dinners until they are no longer "cute".

Pimm's Cup   Beer

Salted Nuts

Melon Frappé or Gazpacho

Butter Lettuce and Grilled Shrimp

Grilled Jerk Chicken

Corn and Pepper Jubilee

Bakery Rolls

Fresh Peaches and Ginger Cookies

Pimm's #1
1 bottle of bitter lemon
(lemon soda)
1 cucumber peeled and sliced
lengthwise into 6 sticks

Pimm's Cup:
Mix in a tall glass over ice 4oz. Pimm's and top off with bitter lemon.
Garnish with cucumber sticks.

Have lots of cold beer for the jerk chicken.

Melon Frappé

1 cantaloupe or honeydew
melon
1 lemon

Melon Frappé:
*My idea for this came from a salad on the eastern shore of Maryland made
with their famous cantaloupes and Blue Crab. A great way to transport
cold soups is in a well cleaned out ½ gallon waxed juice container.*
Take 1 **very sweet** melon, cantaloupe or honey dew, and peel, then purée
in the blender, ½ at a time, with juice of a ½ lemon for each batch. Chill.

½ cup chopped parsley
½ cup chopped cilantro
1 small jalapeño
1 lime
½ cup crab or bay shrimp

Salsa:
Prepare a salsa of parsley, cilantro and a small piece of the hot pepper
seeded and chopped. The salsa may be made the day before. Mix at the
last second with juice of a lime and baby shrimp or crab. Put 1 heaping
tablespoon of the mix on top of each serving of soup.

*For cantaloupe I like to use crab, for honeydew I prefer to use shrimp.
When you mix the lime juice with the seafood too soon it gets tough.*

If you can not find REALLY good melon make this Gazpacho.

3 cucumbers
1 yellow pepper
4 large tomatoes
1 sweet onion
1 hot pepper, i.e. jalapeño
1 T olive oil
juice of a lime
1 12 oz. can vegetable/tomato
juice if needed
salt and pepper

Gazpacho:
To peel tomatoes bring a small pot of water to boil. Cut a shallow X incision in the skin the size of a quarter. Immerse prepared tomato in the water for 5-10 seconds with a slotted spoon. The skin should start to pull away. If the skin is fast, you may re-immerse for another 5-10 seconds. Be careful not to **cook** the tomato. Once peeled, seed and chop. Peel, seed and chop cucumbers. Finely chop yellow pepper and onion; seed and mince hot pepper. Toss all in a reactive proof bowl and add the lime juice, oil, salt and pepper. You may add vegetable/tomato juice if you need more liquid. Refrigerate for 4 hours for flavors to meld.

3 medium peeled shrimp per
person (about 1 lb.)
1 head boston lettuce
1 recipe Ranch Dressing*

Grilled Shrimp:
Earlier in the day when you grill the chicken, grill shrimp for 3-4 minutes until pink; let everyone place shrimp individually in small lettuce leaves. Serve with homemade Ranch Dressing* transported in a plastic condiment bottle.

12 skin on leg and thigh
quarters of chicken

Our son Adam is a master BBQ guy. He likes his friend "Doctor Dread's" paste which is a HOT HOT Jamaican Paste. If you make the paste yourself, you can adjust the "hot" factor.

Jerk Paste:
8 green onions
2 Habanero peppers
2 cloves garlic
4 T olive oil
4 T lime juice
1 T thyme
1 T allspice
3 T brown sugar
1 T each salt and pepper

Grilled Jerk Chicken: (pictured on page 48)
To mitigate the heat factor seed the peppers or use just 1. Process everything in a processor until a thick paste forms.

The night before, rub jerk paste under and on top of the skin of the chicken pieces.

That day, BBQ over medium heat skin side up 15 minutes; turn over and cook 10 minutes more. At this point cut the quarters into pieces and then cook on indirect heat for another 15-20 minutes. The internal temperature should be 180°.

10 ears corn
2 chopped red peppers
2 T olive oil
1 T rice vinegar
salt and pepper to taste

Corn and Red Pepper Jubilee: (pictured on page 48)
Cut fresh corn off the cob and sauté the corn and the peppers in oil, until just cooked, about 3 minutes; add vinegar, salt and pepper and stir. This is good hot or at room temperature.

¾ cup butter
1 cup white sugar
4 T molasses
1 large egg
1 ½ cups flour
¾ t baking soda
1 ½ t ginger
1 t ground cloves
¼ t nutmeg
extra turbinado sugar for sprinkling

6 fresh peaches

Ginger Cookies:
Cream butter and sugar; add molasses and egg; mix well. Sift flour with baking soda, ginger, cloves and a pinch of salt; mix into sugar and butter. The dough will be soft. Drop 1½ T size balls onto parchment covered cookie sheet. Space 2-3 inches apart. Bake at 375˚ 5-7 minutes, watching that they do not burn. Remove from oven and sprinkle with extra Turbinado sugar. Cool and store in an airtight container. These will keep for a week.

Cut peaches into quarters and serve on a plate. Pass the cookies.

Fall Barbeque

For 12

This is a California rooted dinner that is good any time. It also makes a fine Thanksgiving dinner. We have frequently had BBQ dinners at Thanksgiving. If it is a Thanksgiving dinner share the cooking! There are many items that may be eaten by vegetarians. Decorate with fall leaves, nuts and chrysanthemums.

Beer   Cranberry Juice Pinot Gris   Pinot Noir

Spicy Won Ton Crisps

or

Yummy Yam Soup

Seafood Salad in Endive Leaves

BBQ Turkey

Spinach Salad with Red Onions

Last of the Summer Vegetables

Artichoke Panade

Orange Ice

Harvest Tart

Pinot Gris is a good white for this meal. Pinot Noir is a medium bodied red.

¼ cup salted butter
1 T Cholula
20 won ton wrappers

Won Ton Crisps:
These are best made at the last minute to pop out of the oven when guests arrive.
Heat the oven to 375˚. In microwave melt the butter, then add Cholula. Cut won ton wrappers in half or use 5 egg roll sheets cut into quarters. On 2 10 x 15 baking sheets that have been sprayed with cooking spray, or on parchment, place the won ton in a single layer and brush with butter mix; bake until golden, about 5 minutes.

6 large yams
2 cloves garlic
1 shallot
1 knob ginger
2 quarts "non-chicken" broth
1 bunch cilantro

Yummy Yam Soup:
Make this soup instead of the won tons if your BBQ is away from home. Transport in a thermos.
Cook peeled yams in water to cover with garlic, shallot, and a knob of ginger. When fork tender, remove ginger and place yams and the water along with broth in a blender. You will need to do this in 3 batches or use an immersion blender. Put in a thermos and serve in a small cup with chopped cilantro as garnish.

¾ lb. crab
¾ lb. bay shrimp
3 green onions
3 stalks celery
½ cup mayonnaise
¼ cup chili sauce
½ t cumin
salt and pepper
2 limes
4 endives

Seafood Salad:
Remove onion skin. Set aside. Remove celery leaves and bottoms. Set aside. Reserve for broth.
Gently mix crab meat and shrimp with diced green onions, diced celery, mayonnaise, cumin, salt and pepper. Chill overnight. Immediately before serving, mix in the juice of 1 lime. Serve with endive spears from 4 endives that you have washed and separated the night before and put in a baggie.

To Serve: Put 1 heaping tablespoon of seafood on each leaf or put the seafood in a bowl in the center of a plate and surround with the endive in spoke fashion. Garnish with lime wedges.

10-12 lb. turkey

BBQ Turkey:
To prepare turkey, cut in half and remove back bones and wing tips. Remove breast portion from the leg/thigh section. You will have 4 pieces.

reserved celery tops, bottoms
reserved onion skins
reserved parsley stems (from panade)
carrot (optional)

Stock:
Put the back bone and wing tips in a stock pot along with the celery tops and bottoms, onion skins, and parsley stems from the prep from other parts of this menu. Throw in a carrot if you have one. Add just enough water to cover. Simmer the stock for 2 hours then strain. You should have 2 cups of very rich stock. Salt and pepper to taste.

Marinade:
5 cloves garlic smashed
1 cup olive oil
¼ cup kosher salt
2 bay leaves
3 sprigs fresh rosemary
1 small jalapeño
3 T lime juice
½ cup orange juice

Take your turkey breast and thigh portions and place in a zip lock bag big enough to hold the turkey parts. Put garlic, olive oil, kosher salt, bay leaves, rosemary, and pepper in the bag with the turkey. Marinate overnight. 30 minutes **before** cooking, remove the turkey from the refrigerator and add lime juice and orange juice. DO NOT add citrus juices the night before as it cooks the meat and makes it tough.

12 small sprigs rosemary
1 lime cut into 12 wedges

Grill:
Grill turkey quarters on a medium hot grill for 15 minutes on the skin side; turn and cook 15 minutes more, then place on top shelf of BBQ; cook 20 minutes more and turn. When internal temp is 165˚, remove from the BBQ. Loosely cover for 15 minutes, then slice. Garnish with lime sections and rosemary sprigs.

1 very thinly sliced red onion
4 large peeled and sliced oranges (optional)
2.5 lb. bag baby spinach
nasturtium blossoms (optional)

Dressing:
3 T lime juice
1 T honey
½ cup olive oil

Spinach Salad with Red Onions:
The day before slice onion and if not making the Orange Ice, peel 4 large oranges, refrigerate. Just before serving mix spinach with dressing. The dressing may be made the day before. Arrange slices of orange if using and red onion on top. Nasturtium blossoms make a nice finish.

Spinach Salad

2 lbs. sliced tomatoes
5 beets
2 lbs. green beans cooked
large bag salad greens
Red Wine Vinaigrette* See Basics

Last of the Summer Vegetables:
If you can find zebra tomatoes, they make a very pretty color addition.
Beets: The beets may be baked in foil in a 350˚ oven for 1 hour. Allow them to rest until they are cool enough to touch; then peel and slice. Peel and slice tomatoes and place with beets on a bed of greens, add green beans. The vegetables may be cooked the day before. Arrange the vegetables artfully on the greens then drizzle with Vinaigrette*.

1 lb. loaf sourdough bread
2 large onions chopped
4 cloves garlic minced
3 T olive oil
1 ½ cups celery chopped
3 cups water packed
artichoke hearts chopped
1 T fresh chopped rosemary
1 cup chopped parsley
(reserve stems for turkey stock)
2 T chopped fresh sage
1 small bunch kale (to make
1 cup, chopped)
3 cups turkey or vegetable stock
1½ cups grated Swiss cheese
1 cup grated parmesan cheese

Artichoke Panade:

If you use vegetable stock instead of turkey, this makes an excellent vegetarian entrée. It is delicious.

The quality of the bread is very important. Be sure your bread is not soft but is chewy.

Up to **2 days before**, toast bread that has been torn into 1 inch chunks in a 350˚ oven for 5 minutes. They should be golden brown. Cool; put in a plastic bag.

The day before, sauté onions and garlic in oil. Add celery, artichoke hearts, kale, rosemary, parsley, and sage. Mix the vegetables with the Swiss cheese. Put a layer of bread in a buttered 9 x13 baking dish, then a layer of vegetables, bread, vegetables. Pour 3 cups of the stock over all. Do not cook in a deep casserole as the bread will be soggy. Cover with foil and refrigerate overnight. Take out 1 hour before baking and then put in a 350˚ oven covered for 30 minutes, remove foil, sprinkle with parmesan cheese and cook 30 minutes longer. This may be transported by putting the cooked casserole in an insulated bag.

2 cups sugar
1 cup water
1 T gelatin
¼ cup warm water
1 quart each of canned pitted
peaches and apricots
8 oz. fresh orange juice
½ cup fresh lemon juice
pinch of salt

Orange Ice:

This has been in my friend Melinda's family for generations. It was always served at Thanksgiving as a palate cleanser. If you are picnicking, save the ice for afterwards.

Bring sugar and water to boil. Remove from the heat. Dissolve gelatin in ¼ cup warm water. When softened add to the syrup. Add sieved peaches and apricots. You can do this in a blender but the texture and flavor will be different. Add orange juice, lemon juice and salt. If the mix is too sweet, add more lemon juice. Place in container and freeze.

Harvest Tart

3 cups mixed nut meats

Harvest Tart:
This is an adaptation of an old Sunset Magazine recipe.
Toast nut pieces in a 350° oven for 5 minutes. Cool.

1 1/3 cups flour
1 stick cold butter
¼ cup sugar
yolk from 1 large egg

Best Pastry:
In a food processor, put flour, cut up butter; (for savory tarts omit sugar and add a pinch of salt), mix until crumbs form then add egg yolk and blend just until it holds together. Do not over process. Press dough evenly over the bottom and sides of a one inch high tart pan with removable bottom.

3 large eggs
¼ cup melted unsalted butter
1 cup orange blossom honey
1 t grated orange rind

Filling:
In a bowl, beat eggs with butter, honey and orange rind. Add nuts, and pour into a removable bottom tart shell. Bake at 350° on the lower rack for 40 minutes. Make the tart the day before. Keep air tight; to serve remove side and cut into 12 wedges.

Fireside Dinner

For 2

A Fireside Picnic, when you need a change of pace for just the two of you. This is a great dinner as every thing is done before hand. The pies stay hot, and the salad will not wilt, so relax and put on your favorite music!

Martinis

Oysters on the Half Shell

Champagne

Chicken Pot Pies

Mango and Citrus Salad

Chocolate Truffles and Strawberries

1 dozen oysters shucked
or
steamed prawns & chili sauce

lemon wedges

Oysters on the Half Shell: Have your fishmonger open the oysters for you, 6-12 each depending on the size of the oysters and your appetite. Serve simply with a piece of lemon and freshly ground pepper.
If you are not oyster people substitute ½ lb. of prawns with chili sauce.

Chicken Pot Pies

1 T olive oil
½ chopped onion
½ cup chopped wild mushrooms
1 clove garlic
½ minced red pepper
2 stalks chopped celery
3 diced carrots
4 small quartered red potatoes
1 whole chicken breast
1 T olive oil

2 T butter
3 T flour
2 cups chicken broth

Top:
½ package puff pastry
1 egg
½ t truffle oil

Champagne will go well with this menu.

Chicken Pot Pies: (pictured on page 65)
The addition of some Oregon White Truffle Oil adds an exotic sensual aroma to your pot pies. These stay hot for a long time, so they are great for this "picnic". Just enjoy each other.

Cook carrots, and potatoes in water to cover. Drain. In a sauté pan, cook in oil, onion, mushrooms, and garlic. Take off the heat, and put into a bowl with red pepper, celery, cooked potatoes and carrots. In the sauté pan add oil to brown chicken breast that has been cut in half; cook for 10 minutes, remove chicken, cool, and cut into bite size pieces, discarding bones.

Sauce:
Put the butter in the pan, add flour, and cook for 1 minute over low heat. Make a sauce by gradually adding broth to the flour, whisking constantly. Cook until thickened, then add to the other ingredients. This may be made the night before and held in the refrigerator. Bring to room temperature before baking.

Pour into 2, 2 cup ramekins, and top with rounds of puff pastry to fit. If you do not have small ramekins put into one 4 cup casserole and make pastry to fit the top. Press edges into the ramekins, brush lightly with a well beaten egg mixed with 1 T water and pierce the pastry all over with a fork. If you have the time, you can make your initials with the remaining dough. Make a little hole in the top the size of a nickel. Bake for 20-30 minutes at 450˚. At this point you may add 1/4 t truffle oil through the small hole into each pie.

1 small head curly endive
1 mango
1 blood orange

Dressing:
2 T chopped scallions
1 T rice vinegar
2 T olive oil

8 oz. semisweet chocolate
2 T butter
2 T whipping cream
2 T Kahlúa
1 T salt crystals

Mango and Citrus Salad:

Blood oranges are so luscious and beautiful. They are in season around Valentines Day, so make a perfect salad for sweethearts. To peel the mangos, use a small sharp knife. Then turn the mango up onto its sharp side and slice down. You should get 2-3 large slices from each side of the large pit.

Peel and slice the orange.

Mix dressing ingredients. Toss dressing together with the fruits and place over washed curly endive lettuce. Chill.

Chocolate Truffles:

These truffles may be made with almost any liqueur, or none at all. If you are not fond of coffee, use Grand Marnier for an orange flavour or peppermint schnapps for zing. Do not use the salt crystals with the peppermint liqueur.

Put ½ the chocolate into a glass bowl and microwave to melt, 2 -3 minutes. Stir in butter to melt, and then add whipping cream and Kahlúa. Harden in the fridge and then shape into 12 balls. Melt remaining chocolate; place balls on waxed paper and pour the melted chocolate over to coat and sprinkle the balls with salt crystals. These will keep a couple of days refrigerated.

Crab Salad in a Martini Glass

5

IN THE KITCHEN

Tempting Tastes

Out of the South

Fall Brunch

Four Good Friends

Having a meal in the kitchen does call for a certain amount of advanced preparation, so that there is not a mess when your guests arrive. The up side is that there is very little mess after.

Tempting Tastes

For 6

For the table, simply put your favorite spring flowers in a low basket. Everything except the veal and the soufflé is prepared ahead.

Cocktails
Figs Stuffed with Nuts & Cheese
Fume Blanc
Crab Salad in a Martini Glass
Pinot Noir
Veal Scallopini a la Vanessi
Pasta with Babalu Sauce*
Spinach
Bob's Super Soufflé with Crème Anglaise*

Figs Stuffed with Nuts & Cheese

¼ lb. chèvre
24 Roasted Almonds* See Basics
24 small figs
thinly sliced bacon (optional)

Figs Stuffed with Nuts & Cheese:
Wrap chèvre around almonds and place inside the figs. If fresh figs are not available, soak dried figs in water to rehydrate. The filled figs will hold in the refrigerator overnight tightly wrapped. If you want a heartier hot hors d'oeuvre, wrap thin small strips of bacon around the figs and secure with a tooth pick. Bake at 375˚ for 15 minutes. Or just heat the figs without bacon for 5 minutes on a lightly oiled pan.

Fume Blanc is a white wine that is great with the spicy crab.

1 lb. fresh lump crab meat
¼ cup mayonnaise
¼ cup cocktail sauce
2 chopped green onions
2 T finely chopped red pepper
2 T lemon juice
Cholula hot sauce
1 lemon

Crab Salad: (pictured on page 68)
Make a sauce of mayonnaise, cocktail sauce, green onions, red pepper, lemon juice, and a dash of hot sauce. The sauce, without the crab, may be mixed the day before. Just before serving, top the crab with the sauce. If you are using pasteurized crab, mix the crab with the sauce. Mound in a martini glass with a lemon wedge on the side of the glass.

Pinot Noir is a spicy, rich, complex wine that goes well with almost any food.

2 lbs. veal cut for scallopini
flour for dredging about 1 cup
3 T butter
3 T olive oil
¼ cup white wine
1 lemon juiced
Gremolata*

Veal Scallopini a la Vanessi:
Veal has been a "no no" until recently when several purveyors started raising "red" veal in a humane manner. As kids, my brother and I loved to go to Vanessi's in San Francisco, sit at the counter and watch the chefs tossing and flaming the dishes. What a show! You could try tossing the veal in the pan instead of sedately turning it over; very Vanessi.

Pound veal very thinly and dredge in flour that has been seasoned with salt and pepper. Heat the butter and oil in a large skillet over medium heat. Do not let the butter burn. Add the veal and brown on both sides. This takes only 1 minute a side. If your pan is not big enough divide veal, oil and butter, and cook remaining veal. Transfer the veal to a hot platter and place in a 225° oven. In the pan scrape the bits and add wine and lemon juice. Pour sauce over veal and sprinkle with Gremolata*.

1 recipe Babalu Sauce*
½ cup grated parmesan
1 lb. bow tie pasta

Pasta and Babalu Sauce*: See Basics

Cook bow ties per package directions. The pasta may be cooked ahead very al dente and placed in a casserole with the sauce. Reheat for 15-20 minutes in a 350° oven.

2.25 lb. bag baby spinach

Spinach:
Put in a pot with ¼ cup water, cook down, and extract the liquid. Keep hot.

12 cherry tomatoes

To serve: put a couple of pieces of veal on each plate, to one side put the spinach on the other put the pasta that has been mixed with Babalu sauce* and sprinkled with grated parmesan. Garnish each plate with 2 cherry tomatoes cut in half.

1 cup finely chopped prunes
½ cup Armagnac

Bob's Super Soufflé:

Our friend Bob LOVES desserts, and this soufflé is one of his specialties. How he manages to stay skinny as a rail beats me.
2 days before: infuse prunes in Armagnac.

9 inch buttered and sugared
soufflé dish
5 egg whites
3 egg yolks
½ t cream of tarter
7 T white sugar

Soufflé:

Heat oven to 375˚.
Prepare soufflé dish. Whip the whites until soft peaks form and then add sugar and cream of tarter until stiff peaks form. In a separate bowl, mix yolks and prunes, then mix in a couple of tablespoons of the whites to mix. Fold in the remaining whites. Pour into prepared soufflé dish and bake for 25-30 minutes.

1 recipe Crème Anglaise*

He likes to make Crème Anglaise to go with his soufflé.*

Out of the South

A Family Party For 8

While you are having your juleps on the porch, grind the ice cream maker. The table will look pretty with peach and yellow flowers. Serve the ice cream and cookies on the porch.

Mint Juleps
Nuts
Celery Sticks with Pimento Cheese
Chenin Blanc
"Jambo"
Corn Cakes
Salad
Fresh Peach Ice Cream
Norwegian Pepper Cookies

Per drink:
2 T Simple Syrup* See Basics
1 tea bag decaf mint tea
1 sprig mint

Junior Julep:
We all have our own idea of the perfect julep, but here is one for the kids.

Make tea with 1 cup boiling water. Cool; pour into a tall ice filled glass and then add the syrup and mint.

Per drink:
2 T Simple Syrup*
3 oz. Kentucky Bourbon
mint sprig
1 cup crushed ice

Adult Julep:
Fill a silver julep cup with ice. Add the syrup and bourbon. Stir until the outside of the cup is frosted. Stick in a mint sprig.

1 bunch celery

Celery: Wash, trim and cut celery into 3 inch lengths.

1 lb. sharp cheddar
4 oz. jar pimentos
1 T horseradish
½ cup mayonnaise

Pimento Cheese:
Place all ingredients except mayonnaise in a food mill or processor and mix but leave some texture, it should not be a paste. Stir in the mayonnaise. This will keep for a couple of weeks.

To serve: put the cheese into a small bowl. Provide a spreading knife for filling celery.

Chenin Blanc has some acidity that pairs well with the spices.

3 T olive oil
2 chopped sweet onions
1 chopped green pepper
1 seeded and chopped hot
pepper (jalapeño)
4 large peeled and chopped
tomatoes
3-4 boneless half chicken
breasts (about 2 lbs.)
1 lb. Andouille sausage
2 cups long grain rice
4 cups water
1 cup tomato juice
1½ lbs. medium shelled shrimp
1½ cups sliced okra
chopped parsley for garnish

Jambo:

Not Jambalaya! Not Gumbo! Not authentic, but very tasty. Watch the hot peppers if there are small children.

Have ready a sauce of onions that have been sautéed in oil with green pepper, hot pepper, and tomatoes. Cut up the chicken and sausage into bite sized pieces. You may do all this the night before.
30 minutes before eating, heat the sauce in a heavy pan; add the chicken, sausage, rice, and water. Simmer covered for 15-20 minutes over low heat until rice is cooked. Add some tomato juice if it is getting too dry. Next add the okra on top of the mix. This method keeps the okra from getting too cooked and gluey. Let cook covered 5 minutes more. Then add medium shrimp and cook until shrimp are pink, about 2-3 minutes. Mix together. Serve in bowls with parsley sprinkled on top. Pass Cholula for more heat.

1 heart of romaine
1 head red lettuce
½ cup halved pitted kalamata
olives
3 sliced green onions
Simple Vinaigrette* with
Balsamic vinegar

Salad:
Break up greens and add remaining ingredients. Toss salad with Balsamic Simple Vinaigrette.* See Basics

1 cup flour
¾ cup fine yellow corn meal
1 T sugar
2 t baking powder
1 t salt and dash pepper
½ cup buttermilk
3 T melted butter
1 extra large egg
1 cup fresh corn from 2-3 ears

Corn Cakes:

Have everything ready to mix at the last minute.

Mix the dry ingredients together then beat in buttermilk, melted butter, salt and pepper, egg and corn. Batter should be like heavy cream; if not add a little more buttermilk. Fry small 2 inch cakes on a hot greased griddle while the Jambo is in the last 10 minutes of cooking. Keep warm. These are equally good for breakfast with ham and eggs. If you have any left over corn kernels you can toss them on top for a pretty presentation.

Corn Cakes

1 cup crushed fresh peaches
4 room temperature whisked large egg yolks
1 cup sugar divided
1 cup heavy cream
2 cups room temperature milk

Fresh Peach Ice Cream:

This was my father's and my favorite summer treat. I always pooped out way before I finished the churning, and he always finished it.

In a small bowl, put crushed peeled peaches with ½ cup sugar. Stir to dissolve sugar. Set aside. In a heavy sauce pan mix egg yolks with remaining sugar, heavy cream, and milk. Cook over low heat stirring constantly with a wooden spoon all around the pan so that no bits overcook. Bring it ALMOST to a boil, until it is smooth like custard. To stop it from cooking any more, pour into a cold bowl and let sit until it is room temperature. Add the peaches to the cream and freeze according to the instructions on your machine. Makes 1 quart of ice cream.

1 cup unsalted butter
1 cup sugar
1 egg
1 t baking soda
2 ½ cups flour
1 t ground black pepper
1 t cardamom
½ t ground ginger

Norwegian Pepper Cookies:

The first time we went to Norway we spent the whole year, not just a summer. The Jul or Christmas season is filled with baking. No Norwegian housewife would ever make fewer than 7 types of cookies. I loved this one, crisp and spicy.

Preheat oven to 375˚

Cream the butter and sugar until fluffy, add the egg. Sift the dry ingredients together and blend with the butter mixture. Roll into sausages the size of a quarter, wrap in plastic wrap and chill thoroughly. Slice into thin 1/4 inch slices and bake on buttered parchment for 6-8 minutes. Cool on a rack. Makes about 12 dozen, 6 dozen if using cookie cutters.

Fall Brunch

For 4

A time to relax and enjoy good friends.

Pomegranate Kirs
Mango Papaya Kiwi
Stacked Potato Pancakes
with
Gravlax* and Poached Eggs
Bakery Brioche
Fig Jam

bottle of sparkling wine
2 T pomegranate juice

Pomegranate Kirs: A glass of sparkling white wine or champagne with pomegranate juice. Pomegranate juice is VERY healthy, and I just like champagne.

1 mango
1 papaya (not Mexican)
2 kiwis
baby greens
Lavender Honey

Mango etc:
Make a pretty plate with slices of mango, papaya and kiwi on top of the greens; drizzle with Lavender Honey. You may peel and slice the fruit the night before; place in separate baggies and refrigerate. Place on the greens and drizzle with honey just before serving.

half recipe Gravlax
or purchase 1½ lbs. smoked salmon

Gravlax (pictured on page 26):
Make a half recipe at least 48 hours before. Slice the gravlax thinly.

4 eggs
3 T cider vinegar

Poached Eggs:
In a large shallow pan, put water to fill to 2 inches below the top, add vinegar. Bring the water to a simmer and then put your eggs in 1 at a time. Cook until they are the firmness you want them, about 2-3 minutes. They cook very quickly. Remove with a slotted spoon and drain. Set on a warm buttered platter in a 225˚ oven until ready to assemble the stacks.

2 lbs. white potatoes
2 cups cold water
1 T cider vinegar
olive oil

Potato Pancakes:
Peel the potatoes and put in a bowl with water and vinegar. (The vinegar helps keep the potatoes from turning a yucky color.) When ready to fry, pat them dry and then grate the potatoes either by hand or in a food processer. Take 3 T potatoes and pat into 2 inch rounds. Fry in olive oil pressing down on the pancakes to flatten. You should have 16 rounds. Keep warm in the oven as you cook the cakes. If you have a pancake griddle this goes faster. These are best made at the last minute so that they remain soft inside and crispy on the outside.

1 8 oz. container of crème fraîche
1 t horseradish
1 small bunch dill

sliced Brioche loaf

1 recipe Fig Jam:
See Nectarine Jam recipe in Summer Frittata Menu page 25

Crème Fraîche and Dill:
Mix crème fraîche with horseradish and chopped dill. You may make this the night before.
If you can not find crème fraîche you may make it by mixing **12 hours** ahead 1 cup whipping cream with 1 T buttermilk.

To Serve: Make 8 stacks, each consisting of a potato pancake topped with gravlax topped by another pancake topped with gravlax. On each plate put two stacks, nestle a poached egg in between. Top each stack with a dollop of the crème fraîche mix, and put a sprig of dill atop each stack. Grind pepper over the eggs. Pass the fruit and the brioche.

Stacked Potato Pancakes with Gravlax and Poached Eggs

Four Good Friends

For 4

We all love fried things, but who wants to be alone in the kitchen to cook them. Just use lots of votives on a pretty tablecloth for your table. This dinner gives you time to be with your friends while you are all cooking.

Vodka Cocktails
Sue's Oyster Puffs
Syrah
Beef Filets
Onion Custards
Baked Tomatoes
Baby Greens Salad with Pecorino
Gingered Banana Flambé

½ cup flour
1 heaping t baking powder
pinch each of salt and pepper
1 large egg
½ cup cold milk
1 pint well drained small oysters
Crisco vegetable shortening

Sue's Oyster Puffs:

Sue makes such delicious oyster puffs that she is famous for them in the city of Annapolis. Have chili sauce available for dipping, although these are so good that your hand never quite gets to the dipping sauce. I happily have these with just a salad for dinner.

Put oil to a depth of 2 inches in a heavy frying pan with straight sides. Heat to 375˚, it takes about 5 minutes to reach this temperature. Combine the flour, baking powder, salt and pepper. Mix the eggs and milk together and then add to the flour mix stirring well. Gently stir in the oysters.
Put 1 battered oyster at a time into the pan. Do not crowd the pan. They will pop up to the surface of the oil after about 2 minutes. Turn them and when they are golden, remove them with a slotted spoon to drain on a paper towel. Eat while hot. YUM! This batter is equally good for shrimp and vegetables.

Syrah is a red wine that matches well with this combination of foods.

4 filets of beef, 4-5 oz. each
2 T butter
¾ cup red wine
4 sprigs fresh thyme

Beef Filets: (pictured on page 84)

Take 4 individual filets from the refrigerator 30 minutes prior to cooking.
Rub steaks with salt and pepper. Sear in a very hot salted cast iron skillet for 4 minutes per side. Remove meat to a warm platter. The meat should stand for 10 minutes.

In the pan add butter and wine, scraping the bits and reduce to ½ cup. Pour sauce onto the filets and garnish with fresh thyme.

4 cups thinly sliced onions
2 T butter
½ t pepper
¾ cup half and half
2 eggs
½ t salt
cayenne

Onion Custards:

Sauté the onions in butter with pepper until caramelized. Divide onions between 4, 7 oz. buttered ramekins. Blend well the half and half, eggs, salt and dash of cayenne and pour over onions. Place ramekins in a baking pan and pour very hot water into the baking pan so that it comes halfway up the outside of the ramekins. Bake at 325˚ for 30 minutes just until set. Cool slightly to handle.

Beef Filet with Onion Custard and Baked Tomato

2 large tomatoes
2 pinches brown sugar

Baked Tomatoes:
Another Sue trick, put a pinch of brown sugar on the tomatoes.
Cut the tomatoes in half and bake on a pan for 15 minutes along with the custards.

1 small bag baby mixed greens
Simple Vinaigrette* with red wine vinegar
chunk of Pecorino Cheese

Baby Greens Salad with Pecorino:
Take greens and mix with vinaigrette*. Shave pecorino cheese on top.

½ stick butter
2 t freshly grated ginger
½ cup turbinado sugar
4 bananas
1 lime
½ cup rum

Banana Flambé:
I make these on our sailing trips in the tropics because they are quick to fix and we always have bananas ready to be eaten. The bananas are also delicious with pancakes or crèpes. Serve these in shallow bowls with a spoon, everyone will want the juice!

In a large sauté pan, melt butter; add ginger and sugar. Cook to melt sugar and blend flavors. May be done ahead to here. Add 4 not too ripe bananas cut lengthwise and then in half. You will have 16 pieces of banana. Sauté gently so as not to break the pieces of banana. When bananas have begun to caramelize a bit, add the juice of a lime to the pan. Then carefully ignite the rum and pour over bananas.

6

FAST FRIDAYS

Spring

Summer

Fall

Winter

There are so many times when you want to entertain but can not find the time. The secret is to get organized by using foods to cook ahead or freeze and by buying some pre-made items from the market. I like 6 for dinner because there are just enough different personalities to keep things lively, yet not so many people that you have too much to do. Remember you are having these dinners to enjoy your friends!

Spring Fast Friday

For 6

Daffodils sing spring; buy 3 bunches, cut them fairly short and put them in 3 pretty glasses down the table with lots of votives.

Sauvignon Blanc

Hummus & Pitas

Dolmas & Tabbouleh

Fish Steaks/Eggplant and Vegetables

Herb Salad

Baklava

Sauvignon Blanc is a food friendly white.

4 cloves garlic
½ cup olive oil

Night before:
Make oil garlic sauce:
Smash garlic with a quick thwack with a flat knife. In a jar place smashed garlic into oil. Do not refrigerate.

2 large onions
3 yellow peppers
1 red pepper
1 recipe Simple Vinaigrette*
made with white wine
vinegar

Vegetables: (pictured on page 86)
Cut onions and peppers into 1/2 inch slices, put in baggies.

Make White Wine Simple Vinaigrette* See Basics
Cut pitas into wedges and place in an air tight container.

6 4-5 oz. firm fish steaks
Japanese eggplant (vegetarian option)
2 lemons cut for garnish

That Night: (pictured on page 86)
To cook on the grill:
Set heat to medium. Grill fish steaks, onion slices, and pepper slices. Brush veggies with olive oil garlic sauce that you have made the night before. Grill for 10 minutes in a grill pan. Add fish to grill, and brush with infused olive oil. Close the lid and cook 10 minutes per inch of thickness, turn over ½ way through. Serve with lemon.

To buy ready made:
Hummus
12 meatless dolmas
1 pack mixed herb salad
½ cup pitted black olives
1 package pita bread
tabbouleh
baklava

or to cook on the stove:
Sauté cut vegetables for 3 minutes with some of the infused oil. Keep crisp. Broil fish for 10 minutes per inch of thickness, turn over ½ way through. Serve with lemon.

Herb Salad: (pictured on page 86)
Mix the herb salad with olives and toss with vinaigrette.

For vegetarians substitute fish with grilled eggplant. Peel and slice a small Japanese eggplant for each person lengthwise into ½ inch thick pieces. Place slices in a colander and sprinkle with 1 T salt. Let stand ½ hour, rinse and dry, then grill with other veggies. The eggplant will take at least 10 minutes to grill. You will need 1 T more olive oil for each eggplant.

Purchase ready made
Tabbouleh

or make it fresh:
½ cup bulgur wheat
1 cup tomato juice
4 bunches flat leaf parsley
3 bunches of mint
1 bunch green onions
2 large cucumbers
½ cup olive oil
½ cup lemon or lime juice
1 T cumin
salt and pepper
1 large tomato
dash of sumac (optional)

A word on Tabbouleh; this is served everywhere in the Middle East. You will see it on the breakfast buffet and at lunch and dinner. When it is freshly made it is so delicious that I can not get enough of it. You rarely see as much bulgur wheat in it as it is made in the States, and sometimes there is none; my favorite recipe is made from the following ingredients:

Mix wheat with tomato juice to soften about 30 minutes. Set aside while you chop the vegetables. Mix flat leaf parsley stemmed and chopped, mint stemmed and chopped, green onions diced, cucumbers peeled, seeded and diced, olive oil, lemon or lime juice, cumin, salt and pepper, and a large chopped tomato. Combine with the wheat.
Sprinkle with sumac for even more citrus flavor. Delicious!

To serve: Place on individual plates a piece of fish and top with grilled veggies; do the same with the eggplant slices. Garnish with lemon wedges. Have bowls with dolmas, tabbouleh and hummus to pass family style.

Tabbouleh

Summer Fast Friday

For 6

Use a summer basket of flowers for your table. I have a hard time using ready made food in the summer with all the fabulous fresh produce available, but everything may be done ahead to make it easy.

Summer Cocktails
Farmers' Market Veggies
with
Green Goddess Dressing*
Chardonnay
Salmon on a Bed of
Summer Greens
Dilled Potato Salad
Fresh Summer Pickles
Summer Pudding

enough for dipping:
cherry tomatoes
tiny baby beets
tiny carrots
green beans
fresh peas

1 recipe Green Goddess
Dressing*

Farmers' Market Veggies:
Have an assortment of cherry tomatoes, tiny baby beets, tiny carrots, new green beans, fresh little pea pods, whatever looks fresh in the market, and serve with a bowl of Green Goddess Dressing. (You may make the dressing days before.)

Green Goddess Dressing*: See Basics.

Market Veggies with Green Goddess Dressing

Chardonnay is a full bodied white wine.

4lb. center cut filet of salmon

Salmon on a Bed of Summer Greens:
The salmon may be served hot or at room temperature. Cut the salmon into 6 equal size pieces.

¼ cup turbinado sugar
3 T light soy sauce
½ t ground pepper
2 cloves garlic

Glaze:
Put in a small sauce pan sugar, soy sauce, pepper, and chopped garlic; simmer for 15 minutes. The glaze may be made up to 3 days ahead. Brush the salmon with the glaze and wrap in foil and refrigerate overnight. Keeping the salmon skin side down, on top of the foil, bake or grill for 10 minutes per inch of thickness. May be made the night before and refrigerated.

12 oz. summer greens

If the Farmers' Market has purslane, micro greens and baby arugula use them for your bed. Purslane is a truly delicious spring lettuce that is used frequently in the Middle East mixed with yogurt as part of a meze (small plates).

5 lbs. small new potatoes such as red bliss, yellow Finn, or Yukon gold, or a combination
4 T apple cider vinegar
½ sweet onion very thinly sliced
3 T dill
salt and pepper
Greek yogurt (optional)

Dilled Potato Salad:
Wash, but do not peel, the potatoes and cook in salted water to cover until just fork tender. Do not use Russets for this salad as they fall apart. Remove from heat, and while still hot, cut in half; immediately sprinkle with vinegar and toss with onion, snipped dill, salt and pepper. Chill overnight. The salad will keep for 2 days, but the onion gets a little limp, so you might want to add the onion the night before. This salad may be served with a dollop of yogurt on the side.

1 sliced baby bok choy
3 cups sliced cucumber
1 bunch sliced green onions
1 minced clove garlic
4 T rice vinegar
1 T grated ginger
2 T sugar
1 small hot pepper (optional)
salt and pepper

1 cup sugar
8 cups mixed berries or red fruits
1 loaf firm white sandwich bread

½ pint raspberries
1 cup whipped cream

Fresh Summer Pickles:

If you do not want to make the pickles, simply slice the cucumbers and mix with the green onions and vinegar.
Cook bok choy in boiling water for 2 minutes. Drain. Add the bok choy to the cucumber, onions, garlic, vinegar, grated ginger, sugar, salt and pepper. Make this at least 4-5 hours ahead; it will keep for 2-3 days. If you like things HOT, add 1 small seeded hot pepper to the mix; remove before serving.

Summer Pudding:

While trifle is the winter dessert in England, this is the THE beautiful summer one. The color of the berries will determine the color of the pudding. When I first had this in England my friend's mother had fresh currants and I fell for the color. I like to use 4 cups raspberries, 1 cup pitted sweet cherries, 1 cup strawberries, chop them so they are the same size as the raspberries, and 2 cups blue berries or best, currants, if I can find them. It should be made at least one day in advance, but do not let it sit in the mold more than 24 hours.
Simmer the fruit and sugar for about 2-3 minutes until the fruits produce lots of juice. You want them to hold their shape. Find a bowl that is smaller on the bottom than on the top. Cut the crusts off dense white bread and cut into triangles. Line an 8 cup bowl with the slices of bread. Place the bread on the bottom and up the sides making sure there are no gaps. Reserving ½ cup of the juice, pour the fruits into the bread lined bowl. Place more slices of bread on to the top of the pudding, and cover completely. Fit a plate on top and weight with a 3 lb. can. Refrigerate overnight. To serve, slide a long thin spatula around the edges to loosen and invert the pudding onto a pretty plate. Patch any "white spots" with the reserved sauce, and pour the rest of the sauce over the top.

Garnish:

Garnish with fresh berries and serve with whipped cream. It sounds more finicky than it is. After you make it once, it is really easy and so very pretty.

Fall Fast Friday

For 6

This is a very relaxed finger dinner, so you might not want to invite your new boss to it.

Gruner Veltliner or Ale
Olives & Almonds
Mushroom Soup
Hot Baguettes
Artichokes
Chicken
Apple Dessert

Apple anything for dessert; apple turnovers, pie, strudel, baked, even just great apples and cheese with a small cookie. A bowl or basket of beautiful fresh fall apples such as Honey Crisps makes a wonderful edible center piece.

6 artichokes
2 lemons (1 juiced, 1 sliced)
2 cloves garlic
2 cups mayonnaise

Gruner Veltliner, an Austrian white wine, is a good choice for artichokes!

Artichokes:

Cook the artichokes the night before. When buying artichokes make sure they are not dried out. The leaves should not be curling and the choke should feel heavy. Trim about 1-2 inches off the top of the artichokes, and cut bottoms flat. Put in a large pot with water ½ way up sides of choke. Place a slice from one of the lemons on top of each choke, add garlic and the rest of lemon to the pot. Simmer for 45 minutes until the bottom leaves come away easily from the body. Drain and chill up to 24 hours. Serve with mayonnaise mixed with the juice of a lemon.

Artichokes

¾ oz. dried porcini
1 large onion
butter
½ lb. fresh mushrooms
2 T olive oil
2 cloves garlic
1 sprig thyme
5 cups chicken broth
½ cup heavy cream
chives
¼ cup sherry (optional)

Mushroom Soup:

Take dried porcini mushrooms and soften in hot water to cover. Let stand for about a half hour. Chop onion and sauté in olive oil until golden, about 10 min. Add chopped fresh mushrooms, chopped garlic, salt, pepper, thyme and butter and sauté with onions. Add the softened and chopped dried mushrooms and their liquid. When cooked, about 10 minutes, add chicken broth, and gently simmer for 25 minutes, remove thyme, then blend in 2 batches in the blender. Salt and pepper to taste. Refrigerate overnight or up to 2 days ahead. Just before serving, heat to simmer and then add cream. You may also add sherry if you choose. Garnish with chopped chives.

To buy ready made:
1 pint mixed olives
1 can smoked almonds
2 rotisserie chickens
2 baguettes
mayonnaise
apple dessert

Baguettes:
Halve breads lengthwise, butter and cut into 2-3 inch sections; place in sealed foil in oven to heat 15 min at 375˚. The bread may be prepared the night before and heated just before serving.

To serve: Have olives and almonds with drinks. When ready to eat, everyone gets a mug of soup. Cut chickens in quarters and place on a plate with an artichoke. You will have an extra ½ chicken to cut up for seconds. Have bowls of mayonnaise and empty bowls for debris for every two people. Use BIG napkins for this finger licking dinner. Pass sliced hot bread.

1 sheet frozen Puff Pastry
½ cup apricot jam
2 crisp apples
¼ cup Cinnamon Sugar*

Apple Dessert:
If you feel like making a dessert this one is fast, about 30 minutes making and baking.

When you get home from work, take out 1 sheet of puff pastry. Let sit 30 minutes then roll it out and prick with a fork. Brush with ½ cup apricot jam. Core and **very** thinly slice apples. Lay the apple slices in rows down the pastry leaving a slight edge all around. Bake in a 400˚ oven for 15 minutes. Sprinkle with cinnamon sugar and cut into 6 pieces; serve warm.

Winter Fast Friday

For 6

This is the ultimate "Comfort Food Dinner".
Use lots of candles and cut greens for décor. The only things you
have to do that night, are put the rolls in the oven and make the
salad.

Cabernet Sauvignon
Clam Spread & Crackers
Retro Salad
Hot Crusty Rolls
Beef Stew
Butterscotch Pudding

Cabernet Sauvignon is the perfect red wine for this menu because it has lots of body and goes well with the beef stew.

prepared clam dip
crackers

Serve dip and crackers while you make the salad.

1 head iceberg lettuce
4 oz. crumbled blue cheese
Ranch Dressing*
1 can flat anchovies
(optional)

Retro Salad:
Cut a well rinsed head of iceberg lettuce in half and cut each half into 3 wedges, dress with Ranch Dressing* and sprinkle each serving with blue cheese. I like a filet of anchovy on top.

2½ lbs. cubed chuck
4 slices bacon
2 cups chopped onions
3 T flour plus more for dredging
1 cup red wine
1 can beef broth
2 stalks chopped celery
2 cloves garlic
28 oz. can diced tomatoes
1 sprig thyme
1 bay leaf
1 lb. baby carrots
1 lb. fingerling potatoes
parsley

Beef Stew:
Cook the bacon, saving the grease. Dredge beef cubes with flour and brown in a Dutch oven with 4 T bacon grease. Remove the beef and put in the onions to brown, about 3 minutes, adding 1 T more bacon grease if too dry. Then add the 3 T flour and cook for 1 minute, and gradually add in the red wine and broth, scraping up the bits; add in the celery and garlic and cook 1 minute. At this point put the beef, crumbled bacon, tomatoes, thyme and bay leaf into the pot. Cook covered in a 325° oven for 1 hour. Take the pot out of the oven and add the carrots and potatoes. Put back in the oven for another 30 minutes. Cool and refrigerate for up to 3 days. Remove the thyme sprig and bay leaf. On the stove top, bring to a simmer. Serve hot with a parsley garnish.

Beef Stew

1 cup whipping cream
3 cups whole milk
1 cup sugar
½ stick butter
4 large eggs yolks
2 large eggs
1 ¼ cups sugar
½ cup corn starch
2 T rum
1 cup whipping cream
(optional)

Butterscotch Pudding:
The night before:
Have at room temperature whipping cream, whole milk, and eggs. In a heavy pan put sugar and ¼ cup water over medium heat and stir constantly until the sugar turns light brown. Take off the heat and let cool slightly; stir in cubed butter and put back on heat. Careful! It will sizzle. Add the cream and milk stirring until the caramel dissolves again. Remove from heat when incorporated. In another bowl put yolks and whole eggs, add sugar and cornstarch. Mix. Add egg mix to the caramel over medium heat and stir constantly until thickened. Add 2 T rum. Pour the mix through a strainer and pour into individual bowls or glasses. When cool put plastic wrap on top of each one to keep out air. If you do not have enough room in your refrigerator for the glasses, put the pudding in a bowl and cover with wrap.
To serve: Place in individual bowls. You may put whipped cream on top but it is not necessary.
Alternative dessert: Simply serve bowls of vanilla ice cream with butterscotch sauce and chopped walnuts.

Date Sandwiches, Tiny Scones and Cucumber Sandwiches

7

FRUGAL FEST

Tea Party

Mexican Fiesta

Family Fun

A Cozy Dinner

Most of us are social animals, we like to be with our family and friends. In difficult financial times, entertaining may be one of the things in our lives that gets eliminated. Yet we yearn to have a party. Hopefully Frugal Fests will help you out of that dilemma. Have your party!

Tea Party

For 12

When you need to thank someone or celebrate, it is time for a pretty daffodil and pink posy tea party. Bring out your grandmother's tea cups and silver.

Tea
Date Sandwiches
Chicken Salad on Lettuce Leaves
Cucumber Sandwiches
Lemon Cups
Tiny Scones
and
Fresh Strawberries

1 8 oz. package cream cheese
2 T milk
½ cup chopped dates
1 small jar hot mango chutney
salt and pepper
8 slices thin firm white bread

Date Sandwiches: (pictured on page 102)
Makes 32 small sandwiches.

Cream the cheese with the milk.
Add the dates and salt and pepper. Spread the date mixture on 4 of the slices; spread a thin smear of chutney on the other 4 slices; place over the slices with dates and then trim crusts. Cut each sandwich into 4 triangles.

1 small whole chicken
3 chopped green onions
1 cup chopped celery
½ cup chopped walnuts
¼ cup dried cranberries
1 T rice vinegar
1 t cumin
2 T hoisin sauce
½ cup mayonnaise
salt and pepper to taste
1 head iceberg lettuce

Chicken Salad on Lettuce Leaves:
This is an option for people who can not eat wheat.

Simmer a small cut up chicken for 20 minutes. Let it cool in the broth and then remove the skin and the bones and put the skin and bones back in the pot. Make some stock to save.

Finely chop the chicken to get 3 cups. Save the rest for another purpose. Mix together the chicken, green onions, celery, walnuts, fruit, vinegar, cumin, hoisin sauce and mayonnaise. Salt and pepper.

Lettuce: remove outer leaves of the head. Use the inner leaves for filling with chicken mixture.

To serve: Place 1 heaping tablespoon of chicken mixture per piece of lettuce.

½ cup softened butter
½ cup softened cream cheese
½ t horseradish
12 slices firm brown bread
1 very thinly sliced European cucumber
salt and pepper
1 cup finely chopped parsley

Cucumber Sandwiches: (pictured on page 102)
Makes 36 sandwiches

Mix butter with cream cheese and horseradish and spread on 6 slices of bread. Cut off the crusts. Place very thin slices of European cucumber on the sandwiches, salt and pepper them and put 6 more crustless slices on top. Cut into 3 finger slices each. Dip the edges of the sandwiches in the parsley and decorate the platter with sliced cucumber and flowers.

1 cup sugar
2½ T flour
2 eggs separated
2 T melted butter
¾ cup milk
1 lemon rind and juice

Lemon Cups:
Makes 24

You will need a spoon for this almost wheat free treat.
Mix in order; sugar, flour, egg yolks, melted butter, milk, the juice and rind of 1 lemon. Whip the egg whites and fold into the yolk mixture. Pour the batter into paper lined mini muffin tins and bake at 350˚ for 35 minutes.

2 cups flour
½ cup white sugar
¼ t baking powder
¼ t baking soda
pinch of salt
3 T butter
1 5 oz. carton strawberry yogurt
¼ cup water

2 pints strawberries

Tiny Scones: (pictured on 102)
Mix flour, sugar, baking soda, salt and baking powder. Cut butter into the flour. You may make these to here early in the day. Mix with yogurt and water. Make into 24 little scones and bake in a 350˚ oven for 12-15 minutes.

Serve strawberries in a low basket.

Mexican Fiesta

For 16

This is a lot of fun food for not much money. If you live near a Hispanic market, go to it for the ingredients; they will be less expensive, and you will find everything you need. Make your table festive with bright colors and flowers. Zinnias and marigolds are perfect for this party. Add the margaritas and the truffles as your budget allows.

Margaritas   Beer   Watermelon Fresca
Black Bean Dip & Chips
Veggies
Santa Fe Ceviche
Pork Shoulder Roast with Tomatillo Salsa
Chili Heaven
Slaw
Tortillas
Mexican Wedding Cookies
Grapes
Truffles

Margaritas: see page 51

2 large watermelons (about
5 lbs. each)
4 limes
½ cup sugar
7 cups water
mint and/or straws for
garnish

Watermelon Fresca:
This drink is an excellent alternative to sugary sodas for your kids.

Cut up watermelon, seedless is easiest but more expensive, into chunks. You will need 12-14 cups. Add to the seeded watermelon, the lime juice, sugar, and water. If your water tastes of chlorine, use purified water. Purée in batches in a blender, strain and then chill until ice cold. Serve with a sprig of mint and/or straws.

Watermelon Fresca

1 lb. bag of dried black beans
1 large minced onion
1 large minced green pepper
1 seeded and minced hot pepper (i.e. jalapeño)
3 T chili powder
2 T cumin
salt and pepper
1 jicama peeled and sliced
1 green pepper
1 bag tortilla chips

Black Bean Dip:

3 days before, cook dry black beans according to the package with onion. Take ½ of the beans and mash them. Into the whole beans, stir chili powder, green pepper and some hot pepper, cumin, salt and pepper to taste, then mix with the mashed beans. The dip may be made 2-3 days before. Serve with chips and cut up veggie strips such as jicama and peppers. You may cut up the veggies the night before; place in a baggie and refrigerate.

3 lbs. snapper or other firm fish cut into 1 inch cubes
3 limes
1 minced jalapeño pepper
1 finely minced red onion
1 bunch chopped cilantro
sea salt
2 T cumin seeds (optional)

Santa Fe Ceviche:

Marinate the fish in the lime juice; add onion, pepper (seed it to remove some of the heat), and sea salt. Marinate 6 hours or overnight. Just before serving, add cilantro. To finish, toast cumin seeds in a dry pan until fragrant. Grind the seeds in a grinder or mortar and pestle and sprinkle on top.

12 (about 2 lbs.) large tomatillos peeled, blanched and cut in half
1 onion coarsely chopped
salt and pepper
4 cloves garlic
1 bunch cilantro stemmed
1 bunch parsley stemmed
1-2 small hot green peppers
4 T lime juice

Tomatillo Salsa:

Put all ingredients in a food processer and pulse quickly. You want this chunky. This will last 2-4 days but it loses its fresh flavors.

8 lbs. pork shoulder
4 T oil
3 chopped onions
8 cloves minced garlic
2 cups chicken broth (1 cup
if using slow cooker)
Tomatillo Salsa

Pork Shoulder Roast:
If you have a slow cooker this is the place to use it, otherwise use a heavy Dutch oven with a tight seal. Cut up the shoulder of pork into large pieces. Browning first in oil is advisable, even for the slow cooker. Put chopped onions and garlic in with the meat, add the broth and cook 8-10 hours in the slow cooker on low or 3-4 hours in a 275° oven.

Remove meat and add the Tomatillo Salsa to the juices; pour over the meat. The meat holds very well refrigerated, without the salsa, for 2 days. Reheat.

¼ cup olive oil
¼ cup vegetable oil
4 cloves minced garlic
3 T sugar
½ cup fresh lime juice

1 head finely shredded red cabbage
1 head finely shredded green cabbage
1 thinly sliced red onion
1 bunch chopped flat parsley
4 large thinly sliced cucumbers
marigold blossoms

Slaw:
Make a dressing of olive oil and vegetable oil, minced garlic, sugar and fresh lime juice. Blend well and refrigerate for 2-3 days.
To the red and green cabbage, add red onion and parsley. Put in a baggie overnight. Slice cucumbers and put in a baggie.
To serve; pour dressing on cabbage mix and place on a platter and garnish with the cucumber slices and, for a festive look, tiny marigold blossoms without the stems. The blossom petals are edible.

9 cups cooked long grain rice or drained hominy
1½ lbs. grated Monterey Jack cheese
6 cups sour cream
3 4 oz. cans chopped chilies

Chili Heaven:

We have been making this family favorite for decades. I first had it made with hominy instead of rice, in case you want to try it that way. This is an excellent vegetarian entrée.

In a 9 x13 inch casserole you will layer in thirds, rice, grated cheese, and sour cream that has been mixed with the chilies. Make sure that the chilies are **not** pickled. You may make the casserole to here the day before. If it has been refrigerated, take out 1 hour before baking. Bake at 350˚ for 25 minutes covered. Uncover and bake an additional 10-15 minutes until hot throughout. You may freeze this, but the texture is not the same.

2 dozen large wheat tortillas
4 T butter (optional)

Tortillas:

To make with butter: Melt butter and with pastry brush, brush the tortillas with the butter; stack, then wrap the tortillas in 2 packages of foil and warm in the oven for the last 10-15 minutes of the rice bake. They may be wrapped up the day before.

1½ cups walnuts
2 cups flour
1 t baking powder
¼ t ground cloves
¼ t cinnamon
2 sticks butter
1 cup powdered sugar
2 large egg yolks
2 t vanilla
1½ cups powdered sugar for frosting

Mexican Wedding Cookies:

Toast the walnuts in a 325˚ oven for about 5 minutes. Cool. Sift together the flour, baking powder, ground cloves and cinnamon. In a processor put walnuts and 3 T of the flour mix. Finely chop nuts. In a mixer cream butter and powdered sugar. Then add the yolk of a large egg and vanilla. Add the flour and beat. Then stir in the nut mix. On silicone baking mats or parchment lined baking sheets place one tablespoon balls of cookie dough 1 inch apart. Cook for 12 minutes and shift pans in oven. Cook for 10-12 minutes longer. Remove from oven and cool slightly. Sift 1 ½ cups powdered sugar over the warm cookies. When cool pack in air tight container between waxed paper. Makes 3 dozen cookies.

Chocolate Truffles:* see page 66

Family Fun
For 10-12

This menu is sooo easy on the cook as everything except the vegetables may be cooked ahead. Kids love this menu, so it is a good "after soccer" dinner or kids birthday dinner. Have them help you decorate the table with fall leaves and fruits.

Beer and/or Malbec
Spicy Lentils
Polenta with Parmesan
Turkey Meatballs in Tomato Sauce*
Sautéed Mixed Vegetables
Green Salad with Fruit
Kitzie's Cake

Malbec is a medium bodied red wine that goes well with the tomato sauce.

Spicy Lentils:

3 cups brown lentils
¾ cups oil
1 T sea salt
1 T Old Bay Seasoning

An inexpensive alternative to nuts and chips.
Put 3 cups brown lentils into a pot with 12 cups water and bring to a boil. Take off heat and cover and let sit 15 minutes until the lentils are tender enough to chew. Spread on a tea towel to dry overnight. Fry in ¾ cup oil and 1 T sea salt and 1 T Old Bay for about 8 minutes. It is best to do one cup of lentils at a time. They will be crispy. Spread on a paper towel to blot off extra oil. Lentils may be kept in an air-tight container for 2 weeks.

Polenta with Parmesan:

3 cups stone ground corn-meal (i.e. Indian Head)
water according to directions
1 cup grated parmesan cheese

American cornmeal is 1/3 the price of expensive imported Italian polenta.
Make a large batch of polenta per package directions and spread out in a jelly roll pan, cool overnight. Cut into diamond shapes bake to heat through in a 325° oven about 10 minutes. Sprinkle with cheese, bake 3 minutes more.

1 recipe Tomato Sauce*

Tomato Sauce*: See Basics

Turkey Meatballs:

2 ½ lbs. ground turkey
½ cup bread crumbs
1 extra large egg
1 finely chopped onion
3 T finely chopped parsley
2 t oregano
½ t hot pepper flakes
2 T olive oil

Take ground turkey and mix together with bread crumbs, egg, pepper, onion, parsley, oregano, pepper flakes, salt, and pepper. Make into 40 meatballs and sauté in 2 T oil until nicely browned. You may have to do this in 2 batches. Add to the Tomato Sauce* and simmer for ½ hour. May be made ahead to here 2-3 days before or frozen for 3 weeks. Reheat to serve.

Sautéed Mixed Vegetables:

1 large red onion
3 lbs. green beans
6 yellow squash
2 T olive oil
5 T fresh basil chopped
1 lemon for spritzing

Late on the day before prep the vegetables; cut onion in half and slice thinly; cut green beans in half lengthwise, and slice squash thinly. Place into a baggie and refrigerate. 10 minutes before serving, stir fry the vegetables in olive oil just until lightly cooked. Add basil to the mix, and spritz with lemon juice.

Sautéed Mixed Vegetables

8 cups mixed greens
3 pears or apples
1 lime
pomegranate seeds
(optional)
1 recipe Rice Vinaigrette*
See Basics

Green Salad with Fruit:
Use whichever fruit is the least expensive.
You will want various lettuces. In a small bowl thinly slice 3 cored apples or pears and toss with ¼ cup lime juice. May be made to here 1 hour ahead. Dress the greens with Vinaigrette and place the pears on top. Pomegranate seeds make a pretty addition.

1 yellow cake made in a
bundt pan
1 cup sugar
2 lemons
½ cup rum

Kitzie's Cake and Glaze:
Prick the cake with a skewer and glaze with 1 cup sugar that has been cooked with the juice of 2 lemons and ½ cup rum. If there are kids you may want to eliminate the rum and use ½ cup water.

A Cozy Dinner

For 8

In the winter, mussels are quite inexpensive, as are apples. So use apples for the dessert and the center piece and add some greens and votives to the mix. Buy the best cheese you can, and have a finger licking relaxed dinner. Add the flan as time and money allow.

Pinot Gris
Crusty Zucchini
Squash Flan with Red Pepper Sauce
Steamed Mussels
Hot Garlic Bread
Baked Apples
Sharp Cheddar Cheese

Pinot Gris is the perfect white wine with this meal.

2 egg whites
2 large thinly sliced zucchini
Cholula Hot Sauce*
1 cup panko or fine bread
crumbs
½ cup parmesan

Crusty Zucchini:

Whip stiffly the 2 egg whites left from the flan, fold in zucchini and a couple of dashes of Cholula; and then place slices in a mix of panko and parmesan. Place slices separated on an oiled parchment paper covered baking sheet. Bake at 350° for 15-20 minutes until they get crispy. Serve hot out of the oven.

Squash Flan with Red Pepper Sauce

3 large red peppers, roasted, peeled, seeded and chopped
1 shallot peeled
1 T Dijon mustard
¼ cup white wine vinegar
¾ cup olive oil

Red Pepper Sauce:

In a blender put shallot, mustard, vinegar, a pinch of salt, blend then slowly add oil. When the mix starts to thicken, add the peppers. The sauce will keep 4 days.

If fresh peppers are unavailable, a 20 oz. jar of peppers will do. Drain the water or if in oil use it as part of the olive oil, and proceed as above.

2 lbs. butternut squash
4 eggs
2 egg yolks
1 cup half and half
salt and pepper
garnish with chives or a basil
leaf

Squash Flan: (pictured on page 117)
Bake the squash: cut the squash in half and place cut side down in a baking pan with an inch of water. Bake in a 350° oven for 45 minutes. Cool and remove the flesh. You should have 2 cups.
In a processor place the squash and with the machine running add eggs and egg yolks, half and half, and salt and pepper. Pour into 8 1 cup ramekins that have been buttered and that have a circle of parchment paper on the bottom. Or place in an 8 cup casserole. Place the ramekins in a large baking pan and pour very hot water into the baking pan to come halfway up the outsides of the ramekins. Bake until center is set; 30 minutes for the ramekins and 45 minutes for a casserole. Remove from the bath and cool. On 8 plates spoon ¼ cup of the pepper sauce into the middle of the plate and spread out. Unmold the flan and center on the sauce. If you have made this in a casserole simply spoon a portion on top. Garnish with a basil leaf or chives.

7-10 lbs. Mussels
2 T butter
2 T olive oil
1 large chopped onion
4 stalks chopped celery
4 cloves chopped garlic
½ cup chopped Italian
parsley
1 T pepper
1 cup white wine
1 cup water

Steamed Mussels: If you do not make the flan, you will need 10 lbs. of mussels.
In a pan, melt butter, add olive oil and sauté onion and celery; cook until onion is transparent, and then add garlic and parsley. (All the vegetables except the parsley may be prepped a day or two before.) In a large pot place vegetables, salt, pepper, and wine. Bring to a boil and simmer for 10 minutes, then add 1 cup water and mussels that have been washed and cleaned. Mussels are ready when they open, about 2-3 minutes. Stir them, cook for 1 minute longer and discard any that do not open. Ladle some of the broth and mussels into individual bowls, and serve with hot crusty bread. Have large bowls for the discarded mussel shells.

Baked Apples:

These are best warm out of the oven, but they are also wonderful reheated for breakfast. The smell is enticing. The apples may be made with or without the pastry; you may simply fill the apples and bake in the syrup for ½ hour.

2 cups brown sugar
½ cup water
1 cinnamon stick
6 whole cloves

Cook over medium heat brown sugar, water, whole cinnamon stick and cloves until sugar melts. The syrup may be made 2 days ahead.
Make Mom's pie crust or use prepared pastry, and cut 8 1/8 th inch thick 6 inch squares.

1 ½ cups Wondra
1 cup all purpose flour
1 t salt
½ cups +3 T shortening such as Crisco
7 T ice water

Mom's Pie Crust: enough for a 2 crust pie
Mix together cutting in the shortening either by hand or in a food processor until the mixture looks like crumbs. Place in a bowl and incorporate the ice water. Do not over work. Put the dough into 2 balls and wrap in waxed paper. Place in the freezer for ½ hour, and then roll out on a floured surface.

8 small tart apples
1 cup brown sugar
½ cup raisins
2 T cinnamon
1 t nutmeg
1 t ground cloves

Peel and core the apples and place each in the center of a pastry square. Mix brown sugar with raisins, cinnamon, nutmeg and cloves, and place inside the cored apples. Bring up the dough to the tops of the apples and using a wet finger seal the dough and repair tears. With the extra dough cut out 16 leaf shapes and place 2 on top of each apple. May be made to here the day before, but bring the apples back to room temperature to bake. Put the apples in a baking pan and having removed the cinnamon stick and cloves, pour the syrup around the apples. Bake in a 325˚ oven for 45 minutes.

wedge of sharp cheddar cheese

To serve: Everyone gets an apple. Pass a plate with the sharp cheddar for guests to help themselves.

Zabaglione

8

AROUND THE WORLD

English Dinner

French Dinner

German Dinner

Italian Dinner

How fortunate we have been to live in and visit many countries. As an American abroad, people were always fascinated to see what I cooked. Pre Alice Waters they assumed that it was all canned or frozen TV Dinners. I could write a book just about that attitude. The first dinner party that we gave in England I spent all day cooking and made a divine Veal Marengo from the Gourmet cookbook with Nina's gnocchi. Our guests were Lady Barbara and Adam Kwiatkowski and Anthony Reginald Wyldebore-Smith and his wife Honor. As Tony was eating the veal he said, "Patsy, you do such wonderful things with leftovers". So much for not serving a "joint" of beef!

English Dinner

For 8

We spent a scholarly year in England, and the last half of that time out in the country with free range eggs, a walled garden with incredible white peaches and fresh produce. Mrs. Lloyd, the cook on the estate was a meat and potatoes woman; however, I have never seen so many delicious desserts with apples. This dinner ends with one of those desserts. The table was set with antique linens, Georgian silver and Royal Crown Derby china.

Graves

Smoked Trout

Sorrel Soup

Lady Barbara's Deviled Chicken

Mixed Root Vegetables

Spring Peas

A Savory

Apple Charlotte

Graves is a French white wine from Bordeaux.

Smoked Trout:

4 filets of smoked trout
2 bunches of watercress
½ cup whipped cream
¼ cup sour cream
2 T horseradish
8 small slices brown bread
unsalted butter

On 8 pretty plates place a bed of watercress. On top of the cress put a half of a smoked trout. Make a sauce of sour cream and horseradish mixed together and then folded into the whipped cream; put some on each trout. Serve with a thinly sliced piece of buttered brown bread cut into triangles.

Sorrel Soup:

4 sliced leeks, white part only
1 T olive oil
1 large potato peeled and chopped
2 quarts chicken broth
1 lb. stemmed sorrel
2 hard boiled eggs

I first had sorrel soup in England. My Polish friend found the wild sorrel as we were hunting mushrooms.

In a large sauce pan sauté leeks in oil, add potato and broth. Cook. This may be done the day before. Just before serving, blend broth with 1 large bunch cleaned and stemmed sorrel. Set aside 4 blades of sorrel. Reheat and serve with a slice of hard cooked egg. Make a chiffonade of sorrel by cutting blades very thinly and sprinkle on top of the soup.

Lady Barbara's Deviled Chicken:
This is a terrific do ahead entrée.

20 bone in chicken thighs
salt and pepper
2 T butter
2 T olive oil
20 T Dijon style mustard
2 cups toasted bread crumbs*

Prick the skin of the thighs and salt and pepper them; brown them in butter and oil. You will probably have to do this in two batches, so use half the butter and oil for each. Remove to a flat baking dish and then spread mustard on the top of each thigh. Let sit, covered, overnight in the refrigerator. Just before baking, top each piece with fresh bread crumbs. The crumbs should not be fine, but a little coarse. (You may make them the day before.)
Bake covered for 20 minutes at 350˚; uncover, baste with the pan juices and bake 20 minutes more.

123

8 small potatoes peeled
4 large carrots peeled
4 parsnips peeled
3 T olive oil
salt and pepper
3 T chopped parsley

Mixed Root Vegetables:
Cut the vegetables into 1 inch cubes and place in a baking dish. Drizzle olive oil over the vegetables, add salt and pepper. Bake for 45 minutes at 350˚ turning the vegetables over halfway through. Garnish with chopped parsley. To do ahead, cook to the halfway point.

5 cups spring peas

Spring Peas:
Cook the peas in ½ cup of water until tender.

8 large stalks trimmed celery
6 oz. stilton

A Savory:
Lady Barbara frequently had a little "Piquant" taste before the sweet.
Soften the cheese. Take cheese and fill the de-stringed stalks. Cut into 4 pieces each.

20 slices firm white bread
1 cup butter, melted
2 ½ lbs. tart apples
½ cup turbinado sugar
½ t nutmeg
½ t cloves

Apple Charlotte:
This does require a special metal mold called a Charlotte Mold, but you will love this sweet. One of the wonderful things about this desert is that the ingredients are items that we frequently have on hand so you will find yourself making this dessert often.
Peeled, cored and chopped apples, nutmeg, cloves and sugar simmered until the apples are soft.

1 recipe Crème Anglaise* See Basics

Trim bread of their crusts; keep one slice for a circle for the bottom of the mold; then cut remainder of slices into 3 fingers, for the sides. If the bread slices are small, cut in pieces to totally cover the bottom of the mold. Dip all the bread into the melted butter. Line a buttered Charlotte mold with the bread, fitting the bottom and overlapping the slices going up the side, buttered side out. Fill with stewed apples. Fit a lid of bread on top and bake at 350˚ for 20-25 minutes until the bread is golden. Let cool slightly. Unmold. It may be served with whipped cream or Crème Anglaise*.

Apple Charlotte

French Dinner

For 6

We had this dinner in Never, France in an old, slightly run down, chateau where we were staying. The owner was a fabulous cook, as we had discovered when we were there on a previous visit. On this trip we had our teenage daughter and son and our son's friend Tod. Madame was cooking that night for the local Rotary Club, so we were put in the living room in front of the fireplace and we were given an aperitif that she had made herself. Potent! The kids got noisy, but not as noisy as the Rotarians. Bon Appétit!

Beaujolais Village
Mushrooms a la Grecque
Crusty Bread
Poulet a la Crème
Salad and Cheese
Meringue Shells* with Berries
and Crème Anglaise*

Beaujolais Village is a French light red wine.

1 ½ lbs. baby mushrooms
1½ cups water
½ cup white wine
1 cup olive oil
1 clove garlic
1 bay leaf
1 T lemon juice
6 pepper corns
fresh sprigs of rosemary, sage, and thyme
1 tomato
6 T chopped parsley

Mushrooms a la Grecque:
These are wonderful to have in your refrigerator. They make an instant party.

Place mushrooms in a sauce pan. They should be the size of your thumb. If you can not find them, cut up the smallest mushrooms you can find to the required size. Add olive oil, water, wine, smashed garlic, bay leaf, lemon juice, peppercorns, sprig each of fresh rosemary, sage, thyme, and salt. Simmer 10 minutes then cool in marinade overnight. May be made days ahead. Drain slightly and add to the mushrooms the tomato that has been peeled, seeded and cut into fine dice. Mix together and serve at room temperature with a garnish of parsley. Sop up the delicious juice with the bread.

Mushrooms a la Grecque

4 lb. chicken
1 whole chicken breast
salt and pepper
3 T butter
1 clove minced garlic
1 minced shallot
1 bag frozen boiling onions
1 T sugar
1 cup white wine
½ cup chicken stock
1 sprig thyme
2 cups crème fraîche
½ cup chopped parsley

Poulet a la Crème:
Cut up a chicken into 12 pieces for serving. You will have two each of thighs and legs, and 8 pieces of breast. Salt and pepper them, and sauté them carefully in a dutch oven in one layer until golden brown. This takes about 10-15 minutes. Remove the chicken, and in the same pan, sauté defrosted onions, sugar, garlic and shallot. Remove the vegetables to a bowl. Hold. Deglaze the pan with 1 cup white wine and then add back the chicken and ½ cup chicken stock and a sprig of thyme; simmer for 10 minutes. May be made ahead to this point and held overnight. Remove thyme. Gently return to heat and add 2 cups crème fraîche. Cook until sauce has thickened, about 10 minutes. Garnish with the reheated glazed vegetables and parsley.

A small handful arugula (or other summer greens) per person
1 recipe Vinaigrette*
wedge of triple cream cheese such as St. Andre

Salad and Cheese:
Dress greens with Vinaigrette* and 1 small slice of cheese.

Vinaigrette:* See basics

6 Meringue Shells*
½ pint raspberries
½ pint small strawberries
¼ cup sugar
2 T Cointreau

Meringue Shells:* See Basics
Mix the berries with the sugar and Cointreau several hours ahead.

1 recipe Crème Anglaise* **See Basics**

To Serve: Divide berries among the shells; spoon Crème Anglaise over the berries. You may instead make it with ice cream. Put a small scoop of French vanilla ice cream in the meringue and top with the berries.

German Dinner

For 6

*We were at an engineering Conference in delightful
Bamberg and the hosts gave a banquet at the City Hall.
The Hall was in the middle of a bridge over the river.
Charming! I was seated next to the Mayor's wife, and as
she did not speak English and I did not speak German,
it was a wonder that we spent the night chatting away.
Maybe it was all that Riesling. This is the dinner.*

Riesling
Fish in Savoy Cabbage
Veal Birds
Spaetzle
Asparagus
Linzer Tort from the Bakery

Riesling is a German white wine.

2 cups of tomato sauce* (with out basil) See Basics
1 lb. firm fish
1 Savoy cabbage
1 lemon
1 bunch fresh tarragon

Fish in Savoy Cabbage:
You will need a good 1 lb. filet of firm fish. The fish at the dinner was a fresh water fish, but a sea fish will do as well. Cut it into 6 portions. Take 6 large inner leaves of Savoy cabbage and soften in boiling water. Place a piece of fish on each leaf, cover with a slice of lemon, a piece of tarragon and season with salt and pepper. Make a tight package of the leaf by wrapping it under to stay closed around the fish and place in a baking pan that has ½ inch of tomato sauce in it. Sprinkle with 1 T chopped tarragon and bake at 375° for 15 minutes.

To serve: Spoon some sauce onto a small flat bowl and then center the fish package on it. Garnish with a piece of tarragon.

Fish in Savoy Cabbage

6 veal scallops, 5-6 oz. each, not more than ¼ inch thick

3 T butter
1 finely chopped onion
2 stalks finely chopped celery
½ lb thinly sliced mushrooms
1 cup fresh bread crumbs*
4 oz. chopped Westphalian ham
1 t dried marjoram

Sauce:
2 T olive oil
2 T butter
1 minced onion
½ cup chicken broth
3 T tomato purée
1 T Spanish paprika
1 cup sour cream

Veal Birds:
Pound the veal scallops until they are very thin. Do not tear.

Filling:
Sauté in butter until golden the onion, celery, and mushrooms; then add bread crumbs, ham, and marjoram. Cool. Divide the filling between the cutlets and roll up. Secure both ends with toothpicks or tie with kitchen twine. The birds may be made to here and held refrigerated for several hours.

Sauce:
In a large sauté pan, put olive oil over medium heat and brown the birds all over. Remove to a metal baking dish. In the same sauté pan, add the butter and onions and cook to a golden brown. Stir in chicken broth, tomato purée, and paprika. When the sauce is blended, pour it over the birds and cover the pan with foil. They will hold here for several hours or refrigerated overnight. Bake in a 325° oven for 25 minutes until the veal is tender. Remove from the oven and put just the birds on a warm platter, leaving the sauce in the pan. Put the pan on a low heat and add 1 cup sour cream. Salt and pepper to taste. Cook until hot, never letting it boil. You may serve the sauce separately or put some on each bird and pass the rest.

24 spears asparagus
1 t lemon juice

Asparagus:
Cook trimmed spears in boiling salted water until just tender about 2-3 minutes depending upon thickness. Cooking asparagus in boiling water keeps them bright green. Spritz with lemon juice.

1¾ cups flour
½ t salt
¼ t nutmeg
3 extra large eggs at room temperature
¼ cup milk
3 T butter
½ cup chopped parsley

Spaetzle:
I fell for Spaetzle when we lived in Germany for a summer, so I bought a Spaetzle maker but a colander with large holes will work just fine.

Batter:
First mix flour, salt, and nutmeg. Whisk 3 eggs with milk. Make a well in the flour and pour in the egg mix. Combine thoroughly and let rest 15 minutes.

Cook:
In a large pot bring 4 quarts salted water to a boil. Turn down to a simmer and press dough through a Spaetzle maker or a large holed colander. Drop pressed dough into the simmering water in batches, cutting off the noodles if they get too long, and cook for 3 minutes. They will pop up to the surface when done. Place into a colander and cool under running water. They will hold at this point for a few hours or refrigerate overnight. To serve, place Spaetzle in a warm skillet and toss gently with butter, and garnish with chopped parsley.

You could serve egg noodles instead.

Italian Dinner

For 8

The first time I had dinner with Dan's Italian grandparents I thought that the pasta was the main course and ate so much that I could hardly look at the succulent lamb. This is a lovely long dinner, the better to enjoy your guests and food.

Sangiovese
Crab Stuffed Mushrooms
Nuts
Antipasti Salad
Rosemary Grisinni
Nina's Gnocchi
Leg of Lamb
Mint Sauce
Spinach Bake
Zabaglione with Pears and Berries

Sangiovese is a light red Italian grape grown also in California.

Crab Stuffed Mushrooms:

24 small mushrooms
½ lb. crab meat
1 clove minced garlic
2 T minced fresh parsley
2 T mayonnaise
½ cup parmesan cheese
½ cup small bread crumbs
2 T olive oil

The trouble with most stuffed mushrooms is that they are either too big or too wet so that you end up wearing them. Make sure that the size of the mushrooms is one bite only.

De-stem the mushrooms and mince the stems; add to a sauté pan with the garlic, parsley and oil. Sauté until the garlic just begins to take on color. Take off the heat and mix in the mayonnaise and crab. Fill the mushrooms with the mixture and then top with a mix of the cheese and crumbs. Bake in a 325° degree oven until the topping is golden, about 15 minutes.

Rosemary Grisinni:

1 cup warm water
1 package dry yeast
½ t sugar
2¼ cups of bread flour
1 heaping t salt
2 T finely chopped rosemary
2 T olive oil
olive oil spray
sea salt in a grinder

Mix ½ cup warm water (110°), yeast and sugar, wait until it is foamy. Put the flour, salt, and rosemary into a food processor; with the machine running, add the yeast mixture and the oil, adding just enough of the remaining water to make a smooth and elastic ball. Put the dough in an oiled bowl and let rise 2 hours until doubled. Divide the dough into 4 sections. Roll out 1 ball at a time on a floured surface into a rectangle about 12 x 8; these will not be perfect rectangles. It does not matter. Cut into thin strips. They will not be even and that is OK and part of the charm. Place on a parchment covered baking sheet. Spray with olive oil and grind salt over the sticks. Bake in a 350° oven for about 25-30 minutes until the sticks are a lovely gold. Switch the pans halfway through for even cooking. Make sure they are crispy, otherwise they do not last. Cool on a rack. These are best fresh but they will last for a couple of days in a well sealed bag.

2 hearts of romaine
8 thin slices of salami in julienne
2 sliced sticks celery
16 black olives
8 rolled anchovies
1 recipe Red Wine Vinaigrette*

Antipasti Salad:
Slice lengthwise 2 hearts of Romaine, then cut each piece in half lengthwise again. You will have 8 long sections. Trim as necessary. Place each section on a salad plate and top with the following; salami cut in julienne, celery, black olives, and an anchovy. Dress with Red Wine Vinaigrette*.

2 large Russet potatoes to make 2 cups cooked
¼ cup whipped egg
1 cup flour

Nina's Gnocchi:
My husband's Italian grandmother, Nina, taught me how to make these delicious bites. Serve with a simple topping of butter, parmesan cheese and freshly chopped parsley. If this were a main dish I would serve it with Babalu sauce and lots of cheese.*

Bake the potatoes in a 375° oven for about an hour until skin is starting to get crisp. You need dry potatoes. Cut in half and scoop out potatoes into a potato ricer or mash with a fork. When just warm, add ½ the flour and then the egg and then ½ of the remaining flour. Mix with your hand, turn out onto a well floured surface, incorporating the remaining flour, knead until it feels, said Nina, like a baby's bottom. Cut into 4 sections; roll with your hands into a 18-20 inch snake the thickness of your thumb, and cut each into 10 pieces. Press with a fork to make a pattern on each one. Put on a floured flat pan. You should have 40 pieces. They will hold here overnight well covered.
To cook, have a large pot of boiling salted water, bring down to a simmer. Drop in the gnocchi; they will pop to the top when they are done.

½ stick butter
1 cup parmesan cheese
½ cup chopped parsley

Toss the gnocchi gently with the butter, parsley and cheese.

Zinfandel is an interesting, peppery, red wine that is good with the lamb.

5- to 6 lb. leg of lamb
6 cloves garlic
10-12 sprigs rosemary
olive oil

Leg of Lamb:
Preheat the oven to 425°. Take one bone in leg of lamb and make slits in the fat and insert slivers of garlic and sprigs of rosemary. Brush with olive oil. Liberally rub salt and pepper over the roast. Bake for 15 minutes and then reduce heat to 350° and cook to an internal temperature of 130°, about an hour. Let stand, loosely covered, 15 minutes before slicing.

1 jar mint jelly
3 T raspberry vinegar
1 bunch fresh mint
2 pieces fresh rosemary
about 5 inches each

Mint Sauce:
In a sauce pan put jelly, vinegar, half of the mint, and all the rosemary. Bring to a boil and simmer for 10 minutes. **Let cool overnight.** Strain and serve with the lamb. Use the remaining mint for garnish. The sauce may be made 2 days ahead.

10 oz. frozen spinach
¼ t nutmeg
6 egg whites
¼ cup butter
¼ cup Wondra flour
½ cup milk

Spinach Bake:
Make a cream sauce; melt butter and add Wondra until incorporated. Then add warm milk stirring constantly. Add nutmeg, salt and pepper. Squeeze all the moisture out of the thawed spinach. Mix the spinach with the sauce. Make ahead to here in the morning. Whip the whites until stiff; fold into the creamed spinach. Pour into a buttered soufflé dish and bake for 20 minutes at 350° along with the lamb.

Zabaglione: (also pictured on 120)
*My husband did not like this dessert as a kid because of the Marsala. And now…..! So if you are serving this dinner to kids use a light hand on the wine or better yet serve them ice cream cones. The Italian cones, cannoli, are delicious stuffed with soft ice cream, most Italian delis have cannoli. This is a variation on zabaglione as it is not served warm. I really like it with the pears. If you don't use pears, you need to **double** the zabaglione recipe.*

6 egg yolks
½ cup super fine sugar
¼ cup Moscato or Marsala
1 t lemon peel

In a double boiler over simmering water, combine the yolks, sugar, grated lemon peel, and wine. Whisk steadily until the ingredients triple in volume. This will take 8-10 minutes. Let cool. May rest at room temperature.

Zabaglione

4 Bosc pears
1 quart water
1 ½ cups sugar
1 lemon

Poached Pears:
Dissolve the sugar in the water over medium heat to make syrup. Peel, core and quarter the pears. Zest the lemon, and cut the zested lemon in half.

Place the pears, lemon zest and lemon pieces into the syrup and simmer for about 20-25 minutes. Make sure the pears stay submerged in the syrup. Cool. These may be refrigerated for a week.

1 T lemon zest
1 cup mixed berries

To Serve: Place 2 quarters each of drained pears in 8 dessert bowls and divide the Zabaglione among the bowls. Sprinkle with zest and berries.

Pavlova

9

SEASONAL DINNERS

Spring

Summer

Fall

Winter

I am crazy about farmers' markets, and no matter where we are in the world I visit them. All those fleeting seasonal fruits and vegetables… so beautiful! It always used to make me crazy in Paris to see all the wonderful fresh produce at the markets and know that we were never going to see any on a classic menu.

Spring Dinner

For 4

Chesapeake Late Spring Farmers' Market

What says Spring better than asparagus, fresh peas and strawberries? Use their colors in your décor for a delicious look.

Cocktails
Pencil Asparagus
Gewürztraminer
Fresh Pea Soup
Asian Mixed Seafood
over Basmati Rice
New Greens Salad
Strawberries and Sugar Cookies
Candied Orange Peels

pencil size asparagus (6-8 per person)

Pencil Asparagus:
Cut into uniform lengths and blanch by dropping into boiling water for 1 minute. Chill.

1 recipe Green Goddess Dressing* See Basics

Green Goddess Dressing*:
Dip spears of asparagus in dressing.

Gewürztraminer goes well with these Asian flavors.

2 lbs. sugar snap peas
1 quart home made chicken broth
2 T butter
1 small diced sweet onion
1 cup fresh peas shelled
½ cup water
2 t fresh tarragon
crème fraîche
fresh pea tendrils

Fresh Pea Soup:
Put the peas in a pot with 1 quart of home made chicken broth and simmer for 30 minutes. Blend in a blender and then strain the broth. Pressing with a wooden spoon, against the strainer to remove the fibers. Reserve. Meanwhile sauté minced onion in 2 T butter until opaque. Do not brown. The onion pieces should be no larger than a pea. The soup may be cooked to here the day before. Add the freshly shelled peas to the onions along with ½ cup water and chopped fresh tarragon. Sauté 2 minutes then add strained broth. Cook for 5-8 minutes until peas are tender. To serve, top each cup of soup with a squiggle of crème fraîche and pea tendrils. If tendrils are not available, use tarragon leaves.

6 cups cooked Basmati rice

14 oz. can coconut milk
2 cups chicken broth
1 knob ginger
1 stalk lemongrass
½ lb. sliced mushrooms
1 T fish sauce
1 T lime juice
¼ t Chinese chili paste
(HOT)
½ lb. small shrimp
½ lb. bay scallops
½ lb. calamari rings
cilantro leaves for garnish

4 cups young greens
2 stalks sliced celery
4 large radishes
1 recipe Rice Vinaigrette*
See Basics

Asian Mixed Seafood:
Basmati rice cooked to package directions to make 6 cups.

Make the sauce:
In a sauce pan, put coconut milk and broth along with 6 large slices fresh ginger and 1 stalk lemongrass cut into pieces. Cook over medium heat and when reduced to 3 cups, remove the ginger and lemongrass; then add mushrooms, fish sauce, lime juice, and chili paste. Add more of this Chinese condiment if you like things really hot. The dish may be held to here. If holding, add the chili paste just before reheating.

Reheat gently and add the seafood. Cook at a simmer 2 -3 minutes. Serve over Basmati rice.

New Greens Salad:
Mix torn greens, radishes and celery sliced on a slant, with Rice Vinaigrette.* You will only need a couple of tablespoons of dressing if these are very young greens.

1 orange for zest
2 sticks butter
1 cup sugar
1 large room temperature egg
2 t vanilla
1 t orange zest
2 cups flour
1 t baking powder
½ t salt

extra sugar to coat

1 large bar semisweet chocolate

Sugar Cookies:

In mixer, cream butter and sugar until fluffy. Add egg, vanilla and orange zest. Mix well; add 2 cups flour that has been sifted with baking powder and salt. Beat until just combined. Take 1½ tablespoon dough to make balls. Roll balls in sugar and place on ungreased cookie sheet 2 ½ inches apart. Take a flat bottom glass about 2 inches wide, butter it, dip into sugar and flatten the balls. You will need to dip the glass in sugar about every 4 cookies. Bake in a 375˚ oven for 5 minutes then rotate sheets for even cooking. Bake an additional 5 minutes. Watch carefully. Cool 2 minutes. Place on rack to cool.

Dip cookie halfway into chocolate that has been melted in the microwave. When cool, keep in air tight containers with sheets of wax paper between layers.

4 oranges peeled in strips
1 cup sugar
1 cup water
extra fine granulated sugar
for garnish

Candied Orange Peels:

This is an old recipe from Lucile Bush, a native Californian born in 1901. I find that the modern citrus fruits have a lot of pith so try to use thin skinned yellow grapefruit and non navel oranges. The white stuff is bitter. These are delicious with this desert. With the same method you may substitute the oranges with 2 grapefruit, or 8 lemons.

Put peel in water to cover and boil 10 minutes. Drain and then do another low boil for 40 minutes. Drain and remove any pith and cut into thin strips.

Make syrup of the sugar and water; cook the strips of orange peels until they become transparent. Cool and then roll the strips in the granulated sugar.

Summer Dinner

For 6

Fresh juicy tomatoes and luscious peaches are the essence of summer. This is not only a wonderful seasonal menu, but it is an easy on the cook menu where most items are to be made ahead. A cool green and white color scheme would be a terrific look.

Prosecco

Tomato & Cucumber Martini Cup

with Parmesan Crisps

Seafood Kabobs

on a Bed of Greens

with Mango/Pineapple Salsa

Sesame Seed Bakery Rolls

Coconut and Macadamia Macaroons

with Fresh Peaches and Frozen Zabaglione

Tomato and Cucumber Martini Cup

Prosecco is an Italian bubbly.

½ lb. yellow tomatoes
½ lb. red tomatoes
2 small diced cucumbers
3 chopped green onions
1 lime
2 T olive oil
1 T coarse sea salt
freshly ground pepper to taste
6 cucumber slices
18 chives or basil

Tomato and Cucumber Martini Cup: (pictured on page 145)
Using the best seasonal tomatoes, peel, seed, and chop separately yellow tomatoes and red tomatoes, dice the cucumbers, and the green onions. Chill vegetables separately overnight. Layer first the yellow, then the red, and then the cucumbers and onions and divide the dressing among the cups. Garnish with cucumber and chives or basil.

1 cup shredded parmesan cheese
1 t flour

Parmesan Crisps:
The crisps are delicious with the tomatoes.

Heat the oven to 375˚. Line a baking sheet with parchment or silicone baking mat.
To the parmesan cheese, add flour and mix together. On the sheet make 2 inch circles using 2 t cheese mixture. Bake for 8-10 minutes. Let sit 2 minutes, and then transfer to a paper towel. They may be stored for up to 2 days in an air tight container.

1 peeled mango
1 cup fresh pineapple
1 shallot
1 clove garlic
1 T seeded hot pepper
2 T lemon juice

Mango/Pineapple Salsa:
Put the peeled and seeded mango along with the other ingredients into a processor then pulse, keep it chunky. May be made early in the day or the night before.

12 large shrimp
12 large scallops
½ fresh pineapple
½ sweet onion, such as Walla Walla, cut into 3 wedges

Seafood Kabobs:
This dish is a nod to the tropics. Pretend you are in the islands with the palm trees blowing.
Separate the layers of the onion. Thread on 6 skewers (if bamboo, make sure that they have been soaked in water for 30 minutes) alternating ingredients. If you want to have a nice arrangement, here is an attractive display. Each skewer will have a scallop, a piece of onion, a shrimp, pineapple chunk, onion, scallop, pineapple, onion, shrimp. Sure to be a hit at your party.

2 limes
2 T sesame oil
1 clove garlic

Marinade: Mix the ingredients and brush the marinade over the kabobs. Be sure to marinate for 15-20 minutes ONLY. No longer or seafood gets tough.

BBQ over medium heat, turning frequently, for 4 minutes.

½ Walla Walla or Vidallia onion
1 bag greens

Bed of Greens:
The rule of thumb for a bed of greens is one large handful per person.
Toss the greens with the Honey Lime Dressing*. Place the kabobs on salad greens with finely sliced onion. Baby spinach is good here.

Honey Lime Dressing* See Basics

Dressing: Mix the night before the party.

This combination of deserts is not only good together, but it uses the whole egg; and it is a do-ahead dessert.

4 cups unsweetened coconut
1 ¼ cups Macadamia nuts
1 ½ cups sugar
6 egg whites
3 T light corn syrup
1 t vanilla
salt

Coconut and Macadamia Macaroons:
Makes 60 cookies.
Preheat oven to 350˚.
Combine unsweetened coconut and chopped macadamia nuts. Set aside. Combine sugar, egg whites, corn syrup, vanilla and a pinch of salt in a heavy sauce pan. Stir with a wooden spoon constantly over low heat until hot; then pour over the coconut and nuts. Stir well.

On two baking sheets, place silicone baking mat or buttered parchment paper. Drop rounded tablespoons of dough 2 inches apart. At 8 minutes switch the pans from top to center and cook for another 7 min. Cool. Cookies may be kept in an airtight container for about a week. They tend to get chewy if it is humid.

6 egg yolks
¼ cup super fine sugar
1 t lemon peel
¼ cup Marsala
1¼ cups whipped cream

Frozen Zabaglione:
In a double boiler over simmering water, combine the yolks, sugar, grated lemon peel, and Marsala. Whisk steadily until the ingredients triple in volume. This will take 8-10 minutes. Let cool and then fold in the whipped cream. Place in a loaf pan lined with plastic wrap, and cover with foil. Freeze at least 5 hours and up to a week.

2 peaches
6 sprigs of mint

To serve:
Place a slice of Frozen Zabaglione on a plate and garnish with 2 slices of freshly peeled peaches and a fresh mint leaf. Pass the cookies.

Fall Dinner

For 12

With so many delicious fall foods, why not use a cornucopia of fruits and vegetables as your centerpiece.

Spicy Pecans*

Pinot Noir

Tomato Tart

Apple Potato Gratin

Cider Marinated Pork Loin

Zucchini

Fluff

Pinot Noir is the epitome of a red wine for food.

Spicy Pecans*: See Basics

fresh ripe tomatoes
olive oil spray
sea salt

Sunny Tomatoes:
When we are at our mountain cabin in the summer with the dry air, I make these outside, but you can use your oven. These are terrific for flans, foccacio, and tarts as crusts do not get soggy with excess tomato juice, and the tomato flavor is so deliciously concentrated. If you have too many they may be frozen to use later.

On a jelly roll pan put down paper towels to cover the pan and then 1 inch thick slices of tomatoes. Sprinkle with sea salt and set out in the sun to dry for the day. Indoors, spray the pan with oil and put slices in the pan, salt. Roast in a 300˚ oven for 2 hours.

Tomato Tart

1 package frozen puff pastry
1 egg beaten
1 T cold water
½ cup parmesan cheese
8 oz. Herbed Cheese*
12- 36 slices Sunny Tomatoes
micro greens or frisée for
garnish

Tomato Tart:
Take a package of puff pastry and following the directions on the box, roll out and cut into 12 3 inch rounds. You want 1 round per person; or you could make 12 rectangles. Brush each with a bit of beaten egg mixed with 1 T water, sprinkle with a bit of grated parmesan, and prick with a fork. Bake at 375˚ for 10 minutes until puffed and golden. These may be baked hours before serving and kept in an airtight container. Just before serving put 1 T softened Herbed Cheese* on each tart and top with 1-3 slices of "sunny" tomatoes. How many will be determined by the size of your tomato slices, you want the tart to look pretty. Salt, pepper and bake for 10 minutes. Serve with a piece of frisée or a very small handful of micro greens on the side.

2 lbs. peeled and sliced local
market apples
2 lbs. peeled and sliced
Russet potatoes
2 large peeled and sliced
yellow onions
1 cup grated Gruyere cheese
6 egg yolks (save the whites
for the dessert)
1 cup half and half
1 cup milk

Apple Potato Gratin:
This is so good. The tart/sweet taste of the apples with the onions and potatoes is the perfect foil for the simple pork loin. This also can be a vegetarian option.

Prepare apples, potatoes, and onions. Mix together and place 1/2 in a baking dish. Layer ½ cup Gruyere in the middle, place remaining mix and another ½ cup of cheese on the top, season with salt and pepper. Separately, mix together beaten egg yolks with the milk and half and half. Pour the beaten egg mix over the potatoes. This will hold refrigerated unbaked for a several hours. Return to room temperature before baking. Bake at 350˚ for 1 hour.

6 lb. pork loin
Marinade:
4 cups sliced onions
6 cloves garlic
½ cup kosher salt
2 cups apple cider vinegar

Cider Marinated Pork Loin:
With meat, the only way to tell if the meat truly is done, is to use a thermometer. If you do not have one, do get one. They are worth the investment.
Marinate the loin for **2 days** in onions, garlic, salt and vinegar. Prick the loin so the marinade penetrates.

Before baking, rinse and dry the loin. Roast the loin in a 450° oven for 10 minutes. Turn down the oven to 325° and cook until the interior temperature is 147°. This will take between 45-65 minutes depending on the thickness of the roast. Let sit, lightly covered for 15 minutes, then slice.

1 quart fresh apple cider

Glaze:
Take a quart of fresh cider and reduce to half; when cool, it will be a syrup. You may make this a day or two before and reheat. Pour over the slices to serve.

24 zucchini
1 T olive oil
1 lemon

Zucchini:
Take 24 small, 1 inch wide by 4-5 inches long zucchini and cut into rounds; this may be done the night before. Stir fry in oil and just before serving add the juice of a lemon. They should still be crunchy. Salt and pepper to taste.

6 egg whites
¼ t cream of tarter
½ cup fine sugar
1 cup grated dark chocolate
½ cup finely chopped walnuts
12 pieces of mint chocolate leaves

Fluff:

This dessert does not hold long as the egg whites tend to separate, but it is delicious.

Just before dinner whip 6 egg whites, left from the gratin recipe, and cream of tarter until soft peaks form; add sugar and beat until stiff peaks form. Fold in the chocolate and the walnuts. You may grate the chocolate and chop the walnuts earlier that day. Fill 12 small sherbet dishes with the fluff. Hold in the refrigerator until ready for dessert. Garnish with a sprig of mint and chocolate leaves.

1 large bar semi sweet chocolate
12-14 nice even sized rose leaves

Chocolate Leaf:

Melt good quality baking chocolate and brush on the vein side of a rose, lemon or camellia leaf, 2-3 times. Chill between applications. Peel off by grasping the stem end and peeling back. They will keep in the freezer for months well packed.

Winter Dinner

For 10

This is almost a diva dinner, but nothing is terribly tricky to prepare, and many items may be made ahead. Make your table look cozy using a plaid tablecloth or place mats.

Dates
Viognier
Oyster Float Soup
Merlot
Roast Venison & Lingonberry Sauce
Acorn Squash
Brussels Sprouts
Small Salad (optional)
Pavlova* with Meyer Lemon Curd

50 dates
8 oz. chèvre cheese
½ cup crushed pistachio nuts

Dates:

In the Middle East dates and pistachios are eaten constantly. This is a good combination. I love any leftover ones with fried bacon for breakfast.

Slit the dates open and take out the pit. Insert a bit of chèvre, sprinkle with crushed pistachio nuts and bake at 375° for 7-10 minutes. You may prepare these unbaked 24 hours ahead without the nuts. Wrap in plastic wrap and refrigerate. Unwrap, place the dates on baking sheet and add nuts.

Viognier is a lovely full white wine.

1 large baking potato
2 onions
2 T butter
2 cloves garlic
10 oz. spinach (baby spinach)
5 leaves spinach for garnish
2 cups milk
1 cup half and half
2 pints oysters with liquid
cayenne
1 t salt
1 t Worcestershire sauce
frothed low fat milk

Oyster Float Soup:

The soup is a riff on Trader Vic's Bongo Bongo Soup without the MSG and the quarts of whipping cream!

Boil a peeled, chopped potato in water to cover until fork tender. Cool in water.

In a sauce pan, sauté the onion in the butter over low heat until soft, add chopped garlic and continue to cook for 4 minutes, do not let it get brown; add spinach and ½ cup potato water to the onion and cook until limp, add the boiled potato, and process in a blender. May be made to here 1 day ahead. Just before serving heat milk and half and half; add the oysters and their liquid and simmer 2 minutes. Blend in a blender and then add to the blender the spinach/potato mixture, dash cayenne, salt, and Worcestershire sauce. You will need to do this in 2 batches. If you have an immersion blender use that. Bring back to warm in the sauce pan, but do not boil. If you have a milk frother, put 1 T froth on top of each serving, and a couple of pieces of julienned spinach leaves.

Merlot is a smooth red wine.

6 lb. rack of venison
Marinated in:
1 cup gin
4 T juniper berries
1 T kosher salt
½ cup olive oil
1 t freshly grated pepper

Roast Venison:
You will find venison at your local butcher or on the internet. It is expensive, so if cost is a factor, you can use a rack of pork.
Marinate the meat for up to **2 days**. Place the racks in a large plastic bag and turn 2 times a day. Remove from the refrigerator 1 hour before roasting; discard the marinade and wipe the rack dry. Preheat oven to 450˚. Place the rack in a roasting pan and brush with olive oil; cover the bones loosely with foil. Do not cover too tightly or they will have no color. Reduce heat to 375˚ and roast for 30-40 minutes until the internal section is 125˚ for rare. For pork, roast until it is 145˚. Let rest for 10 minutes as you make a sauce with the bits in the pan.

3 T flour
1 cup orange juice
½ cup lingonberry jelly
3 T grated orange rind
1 cup red wine

Lingonberry Sauce:
From the roasting pan, pour off all but 3 T of the fat and, over medium heat, add flour; cook the flour 1 minute. Add orange juice, lingonberry jelly, orange rind and cook until thickened. Then add red wine and bring just to a boil. Serve over the sliced rack.

3 acorn squash

Acorn Squash:
Cut squash crosswise into 1½ inch thick circles. You will need 10 circle pieces. Cut off the ends, you may save them to eat later. You need a large serrated knife to cut through the thick skin of the squash. Actually, a clean hack saw works very well. In an ovenproof pan, put the circles down and prick the insides with a fork; put in enough water to come halfway up the sides of the squash. Put foil over the squash. May be held here several hours; bake at 350˚ for 1 hour until just soft.
If you do not want to make the circles simply cut the squash in half and roast, then scoop out and mash. It will not be as elegant a presentation.

10 cups thinly sliced sprouts
½ cup chopped pancetta
2 T butter
1 lemon juiced to make 3 T

Brussels Sprouts:
You may slice the sprouts the day before. Stir fry in butter and pancetta for 5-7 minutes. Toss with 3 T lemon juice just before serving. If you add the juice too soon the sprouts will lose their lively color.

To serve: Center a circle of the squash on each plate. In the cavity of the squash place brussel sprouts. Place 2 ribs across each other on top of the squash. Pour sauce over ribs.

1 head Boston lettuce
1 head frisée
½ head red lettuce
10 crostini
1 recipe Simple Vinaigrette*
See Basics
1 recipe Meringue Pavlova*
See Basics

Small Salad:
This is a palate cleanser salad. On 10 small plates place a Boston lettuce leaf, a piece of frisée, and some cut up red leaf lettuce. Dress with a Simple Vinaigrette*. Serve with a piece of warmed crostini. If you want to add cheese, a Humbolt Fog would be good with this.

Pavlova: (pictured on page 138)
I got this New Zealand Pavlova recipe from Anna Maria. She just used whipped cream and, of course, kiwi fruits for her décor.
The meringue may be kept in an air tight container for 24 hours.

6 T unsalted butter
6 T sugar
3 extra large egg yolks
5 T Meyer lemon juice or 3 T fresh lemon juice

Meyer Lemon Curd:
Meyer lemons are at their peak in the winter.
In the top of a double boiler, put cut up unsalted butter, sugar, egg yolks at room temperature, and lemon juice. Cook stirring until the mixture thickens, about 6 minutes. Pour through a sieve into a 1 cup glass jar. The curd will keep about a month refrigerated.

½ pint whipping cream
1 box raspberries
1 box blueberries
grated lemon zest from a
Meyer Lemon for garnish

To assemble: 2 hours before serving spread curd on top of the meringue. (This also hides the cracks that occur.) Set aside.

Right before serving: Whip cream until soft peaks form. Pipe the cream around the edges.
Place raspberries and blueberries on top and garnish with some grated lemon zest.

Shrimp Quenelles

10

DIVA DINNERS

Good Friends

Summer Chic

Harvest

Over the Top

Ah the Diva Dinners! They are work, but oh the rewards! Every year we would put on one of these dinners at Christmas time. They were always black tie affairs. I have to admit they became a coveted invitation and were well worth the effort.

Good Friends

For 6

Although this is a Diva Dinner there are only 6 guests so this should be a relaxed good time with one delicious food following another! Pretend you are in Europe where the dinners last for HOURS. Try to cook as many things ahead as possible. Make the grapes part of your centerpiece with some variegated ivy.

Cocktails
Cocktail Mix
Chenin Blanc
Stuffed Mussels
Beet and Orange Soup
Sangiovese
Green Beans
Cannelloni with Two Sauces
Cynthia's Praline Brownies
Green Grapes

½ lb. Roasted Almonds*
½ lb. seedless yellow raisins
½ lb. mixed pitted olives (the smallest varieties work best)
1 lemon
sea salt
pepper

Cocktail Mix:

This is best freshly mixed, but you may have all the ingredients ready to mix. You may make these the night before without the almonds, add them just before serving. Serve in a small bowl for each guest. Don't forget the cocktail napkins!

Mix the almonds, raisins, and drained olives. Grate the lemon peel and juice the lemon; add to the mix with good amount of freshly ground salt and pepper.

Chenin Blanc is a good white wine for the mussels.

2 ½ lbs. mussels
(you need 36 mussels)
½ cup chopped onion
1 clove minced
2 T butter
2 T dill
2 T parsley
1 cup fresh bread crumbs*
2 T olive oil

Stuffed Mussels:

If you do not want to make this a separate course, serve as a hors d'oeuvre. It is a little messier than at the table but these ARE good friends. Serve on small plates with little oyster forks.

In the morning, clean the mussels, and discard any with broken shells. Place the mussels on a baking sheet in a 450° oven until they open, about 3 minutes. Discard any that do not open. Take out and cool; loosen mussels from their shells, saving the juice from the mussels, throw out top half of the shell, and place mussels in their half shell back on the baking sheet.

In a sauté pan, cook onions and garlic in butter with chopped dill and parsley, salt and pepper; then add fresh bread crumbs, mussel juice and olive oil. Stir well to get slightly browned. Place some crumbs on each loosened mussel in its shell. Cover with foil, and refrigerate. Just before serving, remove foil and bake in 450° oven for 5-6 minutes until the crumbs are crispy. Serve hot. Makes about 6 per person.

6 red beets
juice from 2 Valencia oranges
4 cups chicken broth
1 knob fresh ginger
crème fraîche for garnish
chives or grated orange peel
for garnish

Beet and Orange Soup:

This soup is a gorgeous magenta color. You may want to plan your color scheme around that great color. Peonies come to mind.

Roast beets in foil in a 350˚ oven until tender, about 1 hour; cool, then peel and cut in quarters. Grate 1 orange and set the peel aside. Juice the oranges. Place beets in blender with 1 cup orange juice and 1 ½ cups chicken broth, blend. Place soup in pan with 1 large knob grated ginger, barely simmer 1 hour; strain out ginger and add 2 ½ cups chicken broth. You should have 6 cups of soup. You may make this 1 day ahead to this point. Heat soup to serve. Drizzle crème fraîche in a pretty pattern on top; add grated orange peel or chopped chives .

Beet and Orange Soup

Sangiovese is a medium red wine and is good with the pasta.

1 lb. whole green beans

Green Beans:
Tip and tail the beans. Cook the beans in boiling salted water just until tender, about 3 minutes.

1 lb. skinless turkey or chicken breast
1 large onion
2 cloves garlic
2 T olive oil
1 lb. spinach
¼ t nutmeg
12 oz. part skim ricotta
1 egg
½ cup parmesan cheese
salt and pepper

Cannelloni with Two Sauces: (pictured on page 164)
One of my favorite restaurants in San Francisco was the Iron Horse on Maiden Lane. This is my memory of their cannelloni.

The classic filling for cannelloni is veal, but for this filling, you simmer the poultry for 15 minutes. Cool. Hand chop the poultry into a fine mince. If you do this in the processor it will be too pasty. Peel the onion, and put into the food processor with the garlic until minced. Sauté the onion mix in the olive oil until onion is opaque. Take 1 lb. spinach, cooked, chopped and squeezed very dry, you should have 1 cup; add to the poultry and the onion, salt, pepper and ¼ t nutmeg. Just before assembling the cannelloni, mix in drained ricotta cheese, ½ cup parmesan cheese and 1 egg. The filling may be made the day before.

1 recipe Tomato Sauce*
6 tablespoons chopped sun dried tomatoes

Tomato Sauce: To Tomato Sauce* (See Basics) add sun dried tomatoes. You may make the sauce a couple of days ahead.

4 T butter
½ cup Wondra flour
2 cups warm milk
½ cup heavy cream
1 cup Gruyere grated

Béchamel Sauce:
Melt butter in a sauté pan, add flour, and combine. Cook 2 minutes do not let it get brown, then add milk, and stir to make a smooth sauce; add cream and cheese. The sauce may be held for two hours on the top of a double boiler; warm up the sauce to top cannelloni.

I like the cannelloni best with pasta but it can be difficult to find good fresh pasta, so I frequently use crèpes.

12 Savory crèpes*
½ cup parmesan

Crèpes:

You will need 12 crèpes*; divide the filling into 12, put some on each crèpe and roll up the crèpes into tubes. In large rectangular casserole pour tomato sauce to cover bottom, about ¼ in. deep. Place cannelloni seam-side down and slightly apart. For a tidy presentation cut off ½ inch from the ends of the crèpes. Pour some béchamel sauce over each one. Sprinkle parmesan cheese over all. Bake at 350˚ for ½ hour.

or
12 5-in squares of fresh pasta

Pasta:

If you use pasta instead of crèpes you will need fresh pasta. I do not like the prepared tubes for this dish; I think that they are too tough. Drop pasta in boiling water for 2 minutes to soften. Divide filling among pasta squares and roll up. Proceed as for crèpes.

Cannelloni

¾ cup dark brown sugar
6 T butter
3 T evaporated milk
1 heaping cup broken pecans
(between 5-6 oz.-and not a
morsel more!)
3 cups light brown sugar
14 T butter
3 eggs
2 ¼ cups Wondra flour
1½ t vanilla
¾ t salt

Cynthia's Praline Brownies:
These are by far the most delicious brownies you will ever eat. For Cynthia to share this recipe was like giving up her 1ˢᵗ born. You will thank her too. Each little morsel is heaven in the mouth! These freeze well, so they are a terrific treat to have in your freezer for unexpected guests.

Combine brown sugar, butter, and milk in a saucepan. Over low heat, stir and warm just until butter is melted. Use cooking spray generously all over a 9 x 13 baking pan. (Do not use the dark aluminum pans). Sprinkle evenly with pecans.

In a mixer cream light brown sugar with remaining butter; add eggs. Stir in remaining ingredients until moistened. (Do not over mix.) Spread over the pecans and bake at 350˚ for approximately 55 minutes, until brownies test done with a toothpick.

Check every 10 minutes during the baking. The filling tends to form a crust, and then nothing beneath the crust bakes. If a crust starts to form, roil the batter with the edge of a spoon so that the crust is incorporated into the batter.

Put the hot brownie pan on a cooling rack; run a knife around the edges of the pan. Cool 5 minutes. Have a surgical glove and a small spatula ready to use before removing brownies from the oven. Invert the pan onto a plastic chopping board. Use the spatula and a gloved hand to reattach any dough that has stuck to the pan. Let the brownies sit until only warm, and then refrigerate them until they are firm enough to cut. Cut into small squares by using only pressure from a big knife. Pack in airtight container.

green grapes from your
centerpiece

Summer Chic

For 8

Even though this is a Diva dinner it should still be a "fun for you" party; if you have a BBQ helper that really helps. The dinner may be made for vegetarians with 2 adjustments. Have dinner on the terrace with the breezes blowing. A chic palate of black and white with splashes of bright yellow would be great for this dinner.

Bellissimas
Crostini with Tapenade
Sauvignon Blanc
Avocado Gazpacho
Syrah
Grilled Cornish Game Hens
Relleños
Pico de Gallo
Salad with Cherry Tomatoes
Grilled Corn on the Cob
Black Bean Salad
Tuilles with Sorbet and Fruit

per drink:
2 oz. vodka
½ oz. Cointreau
4 oz. blood orange soda
chopped ice
lime slice

12 extra large pimento
stuffed olives
24 large pitted black olives
2 t rinsed capers
1 clove garlic
1 T olive oil
zest from 1 lemon
1 T lemon juice
1 t pepper
crostini

4 cups cucumber peeled and
chopped
4 cups chicken/or vegetable
broth
1 bunch stemmed cilantro
2 limes
½ cup minced red onion
2 large ripe avocados

Bellissimas:
Blood orange soda is so refreshing on a hot summer day.
Fill a tall glass with ice and add vodka, Cointreau, and soda. Garnish with a slice of lime.

Tapenade:
In the food processor chop, but do not make a paste, the olives, garlic and capers and pulse in the oil, pepper, juice and zest of the lemon. The tapenade may be made 2 days ahead. Spread on the crostini.

Sauvignon Blanc is my favorite food friendly white wine.

Avocado Gazpacho:
Use vegetable broth for a vegetarian version.
The day before, place in a blender the cucumber, broth, cilantro, 4 T lime juice. Chill. Put the red onion in a baggie.

To serve: In the blender, place the broth, peeled and seeded avocados, and extra lime juice to taste. Pulse to blend, until it is still just a little chunky. Serve in a small glass and garnish with a sprig of cilantro and the red onion.

Syrah is a red wine that complements the spices in this menu.

6 game hens, quartered
3 lemons juiced
2 T cumin
salt and pepper
1 bunch flat leaf parsley
2 limes

Grilled Cornish Game Hens:
Rub hens with lemon juice, cumin, salt and pepper. Marinate for 1 hour; grill on medium heat for 10 minutes bone side down. Turn over to cook skin side down for 10 minutes. Move to upper rack for 20 minutes; or bake in a 350° oven for 35 minutes. Place on a platter, and garnish with parsley and lime wedges.

Grilled Hens, Corn and Relleños

1 jicama peeled and chopped
3 oranges peeled and chopped
1 cup cilantro leaves chopped
1 cup red onion chopped
1 small hot chili seeded and chopped (jalapeño)
juice of 2 limes

Pico de Gallo:
I am mad for this Baja version of Pico de Gallo. On the streets they sell freshly peeled oranges with a hot sauce-so good. It sounds strange but it is amazingly delicious on a hot day.

Mix all ingredients together earlier. Chill for at least an hour.

168

8 large Poblano peppers
1 onion chopped
2 T olive oil
2 cups grated Mexican cheese
1 cup yellow raisins

Relleños:

For vegetarian entrées have 2 peppers each.

The day before, grill the peppers until they blister, about 7 minutes, turning frequently. If you have a gas stove, you may do this over the flame from the stove. Place them in a paper bag and when cool enough to handle, scrape the skin off. Leaving the stem on, make a slit in the chilies so that you can stuff them. Remove the hot seeds. Remember, the seeds are the hot part, so take them all out. Make a stuffing with the onion that has been sautéed in oil; cool then add onions to the cheese, and raisins. Make the filling the day before and gently stuff the peppers not too full. Cover the peppers with foil. Refrigerate. Take out 1 hour before cooking. Grill with the open side up over indirect heat for 10 minutes until cheese melts, or cook in the oven for 10-13 minutes, until the cheese is melted and pepper is hot.

2 heads romaine
1 basket multi colored cherry tomatoes
Vinaigrette*

Salad with Cherry Tomatoes:

Take 8 outside leaves and save for the bean salad. Cut up the rest of the romaine and toss with Vinaigrette*. Cut cherry tomatoes in half, and place them on the top of the salad.

8-16 ears corn
8 T salted butter
½ T pepper
½ bunch chopped flat leaf parsley

Grilled Corn on the Cob:

Take 8-16 ears (depending on appetites and the size of the corn) of the freshest corn you can find and soak them in water for 30 minutes. Pull back the husks keeping them intact, remove the silk and spread with butter mixed with pepper and parsley. The butter may be made a couple of days ahead; double the amount for 16 ears. Fold the husks back around the corn. They will hold here in a cool place for a couple of hours. Grill on low heat for 20 minutes turning frequently. Serve hot. You may, of course, cook the corn in a pot of boiling water and serve with the parsley butter accompaniment.

1 lb. beans
6 stalks sliced celery
Red Wine Vinaigrette*

Black Bean Salad:

2 days before, cook the beans according to the package directions. Mix the beans and celery with simple red wine vinaigrette. Place in a bowl lined with romaine leaves from the salad.

¼ lb. butter
½ cup sugar
½ cup light corn syrup
½ cup plus 1 T flour
1 cup chopped pecans or
walnuts
2 t vanilla

1 quart mango sorbet
2-3 cups seasonal fruit

Tuilles:
These can be tricky to get right the first time, you must have patience, but they are well worth the effort.
Heat the oven to 325°.
Melt butter in a sauce pan over low heat, and then add brown sugar and corn syrup. Stirring constantly, bring to a full boil. Remove from the heat and stir in flour and chopped nuts. When blended add vanilla.
The best way to cook these is on buttered parchment. The pans need to be thin and flat. Making 2 at a time spread 2-3 T batter into 3-4 inch circle. The Tuilles need to be 8 inches away from each other, and 4 inches away from the edges. Bake until golden brown about 12 minutes. Let cool 1 ½ minutes and gently, with a thin metal spatula remove cookie and carefully drape over a glass that has a 2-3 inch bottom. Shape into a basket. If the Tuilles become too firm, reheat and try again. Let them cool for 2 minutes and remove. These may be kept for 1 week in an air tight container, though they are best if used within 2 days.
Makes 8-12 Tuilles.

Tuilles with Sorbet and Fruit

Harvest

For 8

This dinner is full of lovely colors; many different shades of red and orange. You might want to use those colors in your table top for the dishes, linens and centerpiece.

Champagne
Onion Puffs
Bay Scallops with Cider Sauce
Fume Blanc
Borscht
Pinot Noir
Veal Loin
Spinach in Pumpkins
Potatoes
Persimmon Flan

Serve a brut Champagne with the appetizers.

Onion Puffs:

2 T finely minced red onion
6 T mayonnaise
½ cup grated parmesan cheese
1 slim thinly sliced baguette

Mix together the first 3 ingredients. Set aside. This may be done the day before.

Place bread rounds on a baking pan. Broil until lightly toasted on 1 side. You may do this the day before. Store in a sealed container until ready for use.

To serve: Spread the onion mixture on the untoasted side of your round. Broil for about 2 minutes until golden and bubbly.

Bay Scallops in Cider Sauce:
Cider Sauce:

2 cups fresh apple cider
1 stalk lemongrass
1 knob ginger sliced into three thick slices

Bring to a boil the cider, lemongrass, and ginger. Reduce to 1 cup and then remove lemongrass and ginger. The reduction takes about an hour of cooking. Keep the sauce warm, or refrigerate overnight, and reheat to serve warm.

2½ lbs. tiny bay scallops
2 T butter
2 T olive oil
1 clove garlic

Bay Scallops: Sauté scallops in oil, butter, and minced garlic. They cook quickly, about 1-2 minutes. Serve hot on toothpicks and dip into the sauce. Or serve as a first course in small scallop shells with the cider sauce poured over the scallops and frizzled red onions on top for garnish.

1 red onion
oil for frying

To frizzle onion: Quickly fry very thinly sliced onions in oil just until lightly golden.

Fume Blanc is so good with this crisp soup.

Borscht:
There are more recipes for Borscht than there are people in Russia. This is my version. I really love the color!

6 beets with green tops removed
6 cups chicken or vegetable broth
2 thinly sliced red onions
2 T olive oil
2 thinly sliced stalks celery
2 cups very finely shredded red cabbage
1 lemon
salt and pepper

Cook the beets in the chicken stock for 20 minutes. Cool and then peel and julienne the beets. Strain the broth and reserve. Sauté the onion in olive oil; when opaque add celery, cabbage and the broth. Cook at a simmer for 15 minutes until the vegetables are just tender; add the beets and the juice of the lemon and bring back to a simmer.

1 pint Greek yogurt
1 bunch dill

Serve with a dollop of Greek yogurt and snippets of dill. The soup may be made ahead and reheated, but it will not be quite as fresh and crunchy. It is best to make it up to the point of adding the celery and cabbage. You may cut the cabbage and celery the night before. Add the lemon juice just before serving. For a vegetarian version, use vegetable broth.

Pinot Noir has an affinity with the veal.

Veal Loin:

4 lb. veal loin
2 T butter
1 large onion
2 carrots
2 stalks celery
½ cup Dijon style mustard
1 can beef consommé
1 cup red wine
salt and pepper

Brown a tied loin in butter; chop in the processor the onion, carrot, and celery. Set the vegetables in a metal roasting pan. Put the roast on the vegetables and cover the roast with the mustard. The vegetables may be prepped the day before. Pour 1 can of beef consommé around the roast. Salt and pepper the roast. Bake in a 325° oven for 1½ hours until the internal temperature is 135° for medium rare. Baste the meat occasionally. Remove the roast and put on a platter and lightly cover while you make the sauce. Put the roasting pan on medium high heat and stir the bits; add 1 cup red wine. Heat and serve over the sliced veal.

1 large portabella mushroom per person
½ t mustard
1 T wine
1 T butter

8 mini pumpkins
2½ lb. bag spinach
1 cup sour cream
½ t nutmeg
salt and pepper

Vegetarian Option:
Mix some of the chopped vegetables with a chopped mushroom stem, mustard and wine. Place in a mushroom and top with butter. Bake in oven 15 minutes at 350˚.

Spinach in Pumpkins:
Hollow out 8 small pumpkins that can each hold 2/3 cup of filling. This may be done 2-3 days before. Cover well. Bake them until slightly soft but not falling apart. Cooking times will vary, but about 25 minutes in a 350˚ oven. 10 minutes before serving, place the cooked pumpkins on a baking sheet to reheat until hot.

Cook down spinach. Wring out the water and put the spinach in a processor with sour cream and nutmeg, salt and pepper. Mix well. Heat the spinach in a double boiler, and just before serving fill the hot pumpkins with the spinach.

Veal Loin, Spinach in Pumpkins, and Potatoes

2 lbs. fingerling potatoes
3 T olive oil
salt and pepper

5 extra large eggs
¼ cup sugar
1 ¼ cups milk
1 ¼ cups half and half
1t grated orange peel
¼ cup Cointreau
4 Fuyu persimmons
1 lemon
½ cup raspberries

½ cup sugar
½ cup water

Potatoes:
Cook potatoes in water until fork tender. Drain. Place in a small roasting pan with olive oil and salt and pepper. Heat in a 325˚ oven for 10 minutes when you take the roast out.

Persimmon Flan:
Fuyu persimmons are very different from what we are used to. They have a crisp taste and do not need to be peeled.
In a bowl beat the eggs with the sugar until frothy; whisk in milk and half and half, orange peel, and Cointreau. Strain. Set a deep dish pie pan (1½ qt.) in a larger roasting pan. Put on the center rack of the oven and pour the custard into the pie pan. Pour very hot water into the roasting pan halfway up the outside of the pie pan. Bake for about 25 minutes in a 350˚ oven, until custard is set. Cool and cover with plastic wrap overnight. A couple of hours before serving, slice Fuyu Persimmons in thin wedges and toss with lemon juice to prevent browning. Arrange persimmons in a spoke on top of the custard and sprinkle with ½ cup raspberries. Just before serving drizzle with caramel.

Caramel:
This is a fun trick to have up your party sleeve. You might want to practice making the caramel. If you don't have a party helper, have a good friend remove the dinner dishes while you make the caramel.

Have the sugar ready in a frying pan. Add water; stir only until sugar is dissolved. Over medium heat melt sugar until amber, tilting the pan constantly, but do not stir. If the sugar gets too far up the pan, use a pastry brush to keep it under control, pushing it down into the pan. Remember this stuff is hot! It takes about 6-8 minutes to become amber. Remove from the heat and let cool, about 2 minutes. Working quickly, and using a fork, drizzle caramel over the flan in a lacy pattern. Let the flan sit for a minute to harden. Beware; if it is humid or damp the caramel may just wilt instead of harden.

Over the Top

A Black Tie Affair

For 16

This is an over the top "DIVA" dinner that takes hours around the table. The table should look as gorgeous as the food; maybe white and green with a blast of pomegranate red. Buy out the candle store. There is enough that can be done ahead so that you may enjoy it too. Get your own or a neighborhood teenager to help with the serving and the dishes.

**Dan's Old Fashioned
Cheesy Puff Pastries
Spicy Pecans***

**Chardonnay
Shrimp Quenelles
Cabernet
Beef Tenderloin
with Red Wine Sauce
Potatoes
Snow Peas and Onions
Jewel Salad
Champagne
Holiday Cream Puffs***

Per drink:
½ slice of lemon
½ slice orange
1 maraschino cherry
2 dashes Angostura bitters
3 oz. Canadian whiskey
Old Fashioned glass
crushed ice
Simple Syrup* See Basics

1 package puff pastry
Herbed Cheese* See Basics
½ cup sun dried tomatoes
½ cup chopped kalamata olives
1 egg
½ cup chopped parsley

Dan's Old Fashioned:
These are always served at our holiday party. Be careful they are potent! Have ready a small pitcher of simple syrup.

Fill the glass with crushed ice. Stir the above ingredients into the glass and add 1 T syrup. Stir again.

Cheesy Puff Pastries:
Frozen puff pastry makes these so easy! Take a whole package and prepare per package directions; roll out each piece as thinly as possible about 1/8 th inch. These may go back in the freezer for a day or 2 tightly covered. 2 hours before serving bring to room temperature.

Spirals:
Spread 1 sheet with ½ of the softened Herbed Cheese that has been mixed with minced sun dried tomatoes. Roll up the long side and cut into ½ inch thick rounds and place on a parchment covered cookie sheet. Thoroughly beat 1 egg with 1 T water and brush some on each spiral. Just before baking, add a turn of freshly ground sea salt and bake at 400° for 12 minutes.

Squares:
Mix 5 oz. cheese with the olives and spread the mixture over the rolled out pastry. Cut into bite size squares, and place on a parchment covered cookie sheet. Bake squares for 10 minutes at 400°. Garnish with a bit of chopped parsley.

Spicy Pecans* See Basics

1 recipe **Spicy Pecans***

Chardonnay is rich but so are the Quenelles.

Shrimp Quenelles: (pictured on page 158)
Our daughter Missy and I made this up, remembering the delicious quenelles when we lived in France. The Cuisinart has made this dish "do-able". Tarragon is a wonderful herb that we do not use often enough here in the States. The dish consists of 3 parts, a spinach base, the quenelles and a sauce. It is presented in a scallop shell.

1 lb. medium raw shrimp
16 small raw shrimp
2 T tomato paste

Peel all the shrimp; place the 16 small shelled shrimp and all the other shells into a pan of water to barely cover. Cook shrimp until pink, then remove and reserve the cooked shrimp for garnish. Cook down shell broth to 1 cup. Strain and add tomato paste.

1 cup heavy cream
2 egg whites
cayenne pepper
salt and white pepper

Process the 1 lb. raw medium shrimp until just chopped, some small pieces are OK; add in heavy cream, egg whites, dash of cayenne pepper, and salt and white pepper. Pulse to mix. Chill 2 hours or overnight.

2 lbs. spinach
1 minced shallot
2 T butter

Plunge the spinach into a very large pan with ½ cup boiling water. Stir until cooked. Cool, press out water and then chop and add to shallots that have been sautéed in 2 T butter until cooked but not brown. The spinach may be made the day before, but the color will not be as bright.

Heat the shrimp broth with cream and freshly chopped tarragon. DO NOT BOIL. In a sauté pan melt butter and cook with flour; add shrimp broth and over low heat make a sauce. Add salt and pepper and 1 t lemon juice. It will keep in the top of a double boiler over simmering water.

½ cup cream
2 t fresh chopped tarragon
2 T butter
2 T Wondra flour
salt and pepper to taste
1 t lemon juice

To cook quenelles: Fill a large shallow saucepan with salted water and bring to a simmer. With 2 soup spoons shape shrimp paste into 16 large ovals and nudge them into the simmering water. Allow to cook for 5-8 minutes until they float. Remove with a slotted spoon to a baking dish. The quenelles are really best served right out of the bath, but they may be held here for an hour. Place in a flat baking dish and cover with foil until ready to use. To reheat; place quenelles in a warm oven.

zest from 1 lemon
16 small sprigs fresh tarragon

To assemble: Place a spoonful of hot spinach on a small scallop shell, put a hot quenelle in the center of the spinach and top with 1 T sauce. Garnish with a small shrimp, a piece of tarragon and lemon zest.

Cabernet is the king of reds. Buy a good one.

2 2 lb. beef tenderloins
2 T butter
2 T olive oil
2 T fresh thyme
2 T pepper
2 T sea salt

Beef Tenderloin:
Caterers love tenderloins because they are so easy, and hold so well.
Heat oven to 450˚.
In a large roasting pan, brown tenderloins in butter and oil, thyme, freshly grated pepper and sea salt. When browned all over, about 4 minutes, they may sit for several hours. When ready to cook roast in the oven until the temperature is 120˚ for rare, about 12-18 minutes, remove from oven and cover loosely with foil. It will hold while you are having the first course.

2 lemons
2 oranges
½ cup current jelly
½ cup red wine
½ t grated fresh ginger

Red Wine Sauce:
Grate the rinds of the lemons and oranges; then juice. Combine remaining ingredients and boil until the jelly is melted. This may be made several days ahead. Warm to serve. Makes about 1½ cups sauce.

3 lbs. baby potatoes
2 T butter

Potatoes:
Sauté tiny potatoes, the size of a marble, in the butter for 10 minutes. The potatoes will hold for 3 hours. Reheat before serving.

2 T butter
1 bag frozen boiling onions
2 T sugar
2 lbs. snow peas

Snow Peas and Onions:
Sauté the onions in the butter for 5 minutes; add sugar and cook 5 minutes more to caramelize the onions. You may cook them to here and hold for several hours. Just before serving add the peas, cook for 2-3 minutes until all are hot.

Jewel Salad

2 heads Boston or Bibb lettuce
2 heads frisée
3 Clementines
1 small pomegranate

Jewel Salad:
You could have this salad before the quenelles but I like the taste "break" before the dessert. Besides it gives you a chance to finish the wine. Be sure you use Clementines or other tangerines without seeds.

Break apart the heads of lettuce. Divide the greens between 16 plates and top with the sections from the Clementines and the seeds of a pomegranate, about 1 T per salad. You may pre-plate the salad and then drizzle with Honey Lime Dressing* just before serving.

Honey Lime Dressing*: See Basics
Mix the night before the party.

It is always time for Champagne! Have a sec or demi sec Champagne.

32 small Cream Puffs* See Basics

Holiday Cream Puffs:
Make the puffs from the basic recipe 2-3 days before.

12 oz. package dark chocolate chips
3 large eggs
1 cup hot milk

Chocolate Mousse:
Place in a blender chocolate chips, and eggs; when well mixed, slowly add in the hot milk. Mix until chips are incorporated. Place in a bowl and chill covered. May be made a day ahead.

2 cups whipping cream
4 peppermint sticks finely crushed to make ½ cup
1 cup top quality chocolate sauce
16 extra large strawberries

To Assemble: When Puffs are cool, open the tops and pull out and discard any uncooked bits. Place in an airtight container. Before the party, fill the bottom of the puffs with chocolate mousse. Whip the cream and fold in crushed peppermint. Top the mousse with the cream mixture. This is easiest with a pastry bag. Refrigerate. Just before serving add a drizzle of chocolate sauce on top of the puffs and on the plate in a nice pattern.

A large strawberry looks pretty with the 2 puffs.

Index

Conversion Chart

Because we have lived and cooked in so many different countries, I have learned to adapt the basic measuring units fairly well. Having cookbooks in a foreign language is a fun challenge! I have a couple of really useful tools that I bought at IKEA. One is a small scale that, while not totally accurate, works for cooking. It has both grams and ounces on it. Another is a liquid measurer that has fluid ounces and milliliters on it.

Until you find one of those tools, here is a chart for you to use.

Liquid Measure:
1 t = 5 ml.
1 T= 15 ml.
2 T= 29 ml.
¼ cup= 59 ml.
1/3 cup= 78 ml.
½ cup= 119 ml.
2/3 cup= 155 ml
¾ cup= 175 ml.
1 cup= 235 ml.

Dry Weight:
1 oz. = 30 grams
2 oz. =57 grams
4 oz. (1/4 lb.)= 114 grams
6 oz. =170 grams
8 oz. (1/2 lb.) =228 grams
12 oz. (3/4 lb.) = 340 grams
16 oz. (1 lb.) = 454 grams
2.2 lbs.= 1 kilogram

Degree Conversion:

Fahrenheit	Celsius
250	120
300	150
325	160
350	175
375	190
400	200
450	230